The Light on Old Cape May

("Sea chanty ca: 1900, sung to the tune of "The Bigler")

The wind it blew from Sou'sou'east,

It blew a pleasant breeze

And the man upon the lookout cried:

"A light upon our lee!"

They reported to the captain and

These words did he say-

"Cheer up my sailor lads,

It's the light on old Cape May."[1]

Sentinel of the Jersey Cape
The Story of the Cape May Lighthouse

First Edition ©1989 by John Bailey
Second Edition ©2001 by John Bailey and Cape Publishing, Inc.
Copyright ©2001 All Rights Reserved.

No part of this book may be reproduced or transmitted in any form
or by any means without the expressed written permission
of the publisher.

Cape Publishing, Inc.
727 Beach Drive
P.O. Box 2383
Cape May, New Jersey 08204

Printed in the USA

ISBN 0-9706480-0-6

Sentinel
of the
Jersey Cape

The Story of the Cape May Lighthouse

By John Bailey

Dedicated to

Frederick Kuhner

June 14, 1927 - August 6, 1999

**A founder and first president
of the Mid-Atlantic Center for the Arts.**

&

**A true keeper of the
Cape May Lighthouse**

Preface

*"We live in a moment of history where change
is so speeded up that we begin to see the present
only when it is already disappearing."*
R. D. Laing

Threatened? Yes! Our nation's lighthouses have joined the humpback whale and the manatee on that not-too-exclusive list of endangered species. Deep budget cuts have forced the Coast Guard to abandon these magnificent historic towers that dot our seacoasts, lakes, rivers, and bays. The Coast Guard can only maintain their lights, and time is exacting its toll on their bricks, mortar, and metal. Most of them are over 100 years old. They all stand in locations most exposed to their very enemies: wet salt air, erosion, and coastal over-development. The Coast Guard has transferred the care of lighthouses to various states, counties, or non-profit groups. These groups are struggling to restore and maintain them in their former glory, a costly undertaking.

The Mid-Atlantic Center for the Arts (MAC) has accepted the responsibility for the Cape May Lighthouse. With Tom Carroll, local innkeeper and retired Coast Guard Captain, at the helm, MAC expressed an interest as early as 1983; and, in 1986 the Coast Guard leased the lighthouse to the State of New Jersey, which, in turn signed a sub-lease with MAC, a local non-profit organization, "to restore, maintain, and open the structure to the public." This lighthouse couldn't have fallen into better hands. MAC knows the problems of restoration, its expenses and its pitfalls. MAC is up to the challenge.

MAC had its beginning in 1970 when a small band of Cape May preservationists gathered together to save and restore the Emlen Physick Estate. The Estate's remarkable mansion, designed by Philadelphia architect, Frank Furness, had fallen into terrible disrepair. A local developer had scheduled it for demolition. Today, the mansion is one of the nation's finest house museums, constantly maintained, featuring high quality Victorian furnishings, many that actually belonged to the Physick family. It is open to the public daily. Membership in MAC is open to everyone.

Although Federal and State grants have funded the expensive major restoration projects, the public has also answered the tower's distress signals. Lighthouse lovers from all over the world have donated money, or "purchased" parts of the lighthouse, such as bricks, steps, landings, and windows. Many visitors have bought items in the oil house museum shop. Thousands have taken the challenge and climbed to the top where the view of the Jersey Cape is breathtaking. All of the proceeds from the shop and admissions go directly into maintaining and saving the lighthouse, as well as being used for matching grants.

Acknowledgments

Nancy Bailey for her patience, enthusiasm, and support; and for rereading and commenting and rereading and suggesting and rereading...

Cape May Lighthouse guides (keepers) Charles Rumsey and Dave Yeager for their perceptive remarks and informed questions. These two keepers spend their time on the front lines fielding questions from visitors every day.

Mid-Atlantic Center for the Arts (MAC) President, Tom Carroll for his review of the final draft and his sharp pencil.

MAC curator, Elizabeth Bailey for locating as many photos from the first edition as was humanly possible. (Everything from the first edition burned in a fire at the old Cape Printing office building and was lost.)

Diane Fischer for her careful editing and useful commentary of the first edition.

Captain Ward Brainard of the Cape May-Lewes Ferry for ensuring my accuracy from a mariner's point of view.

The family and descendants of the last keeper of the light, Mr. Harry H. Palmer, for sharing their family history with me. Specifically the following: the late Mrs. Ada Palmer Givens, daughter, for her interest, stories, and personal photographs of the lighthouse and its crew from 1924 through 1935. Mayhugh Tees, granddaughter, for arranging interviews and locating missing family photos.

H. Gerald MacDonald for his enthusiasm in sharing his amazing collection of antique photos and maps of the lighthouse, South Cape May, and Cape May Point.

Robert Elwell, Sr. for sharing his postcard collection with me.

Everyone who loves and supports this lighthouse in any small way that they can.

And finally, Bernard Haas, publisher, for prodding me into beginning the long and arduous task of producing this second edition.

TABLE OF CONTENTS

LIGHTHOUSES OF CAPE MAY
- Before 1823 ....**10**
- 1823 Lighthouse..**13**
- 1847 Lighthouse..**15**
- 1859 Lighthouse..**18**

A TOUR OF THE LIGHTHOUSE
- Double Walls..**26**
- Spiral Stairway...**27**
- Telephone System..**29**
- Lantern 11..**31**
- Fresnel Lens...**33**
- Lamps **35**
- The Current Beacon...**37**

A TOUR OF THE GROUNDS
- Property..**40**
- Buildings...**45**
  - Keepers' Dwellings..**45**
  - Oil House...**47**
  - Earlier Buildings..**48**

KEEPERS OF THE LIGHT
- Evolution Of The Keeper..**49**
  - Lighthouse Board Investigation...**50**
  - Developing the Proper Keeper...**50**
  - Job Description and Wages...**51**
  - Cape May's Keepers...**52**

AFTER THE KEEPERS LEFT
- World War II..**57**
- Post War Coast Guard..**59**
- The Restoration of the Lighthouse..**61**

EPILOGUE..**73**
APPENDIX A Cape May Lighthouse at a Glance: Chronology **78**
- Geography..**84**
APPENDIX B U.S. Lighthouse Administration...**85**
APPENDIX C Inspection Report, Cape May, June 25, 1851 — 4 p.m.....**88**
APPENDIX D Fourth District Engineers Report, 20 March 1878...........**90**
APPENDIX E Map of Cape May Point Showing Erosion and
Locations of All Three Lighthouses..**93**
APPENDIX F Keepers...**94**
APPENDIX G Historical Name..**96**
APPENDIX H A Chronology of Lighthouses...**98**
LETTER OF RECOMMENDATION - 1828 ....**101**
APPENDIX I Lighthouses of New Jersey and the Delaware Bay..........**102**
HIGHLIGHTS FOR NEW JERSEY LIGHTHOUSES............................**111**
INDEX **112**

 *Lighthouses of Cape May*

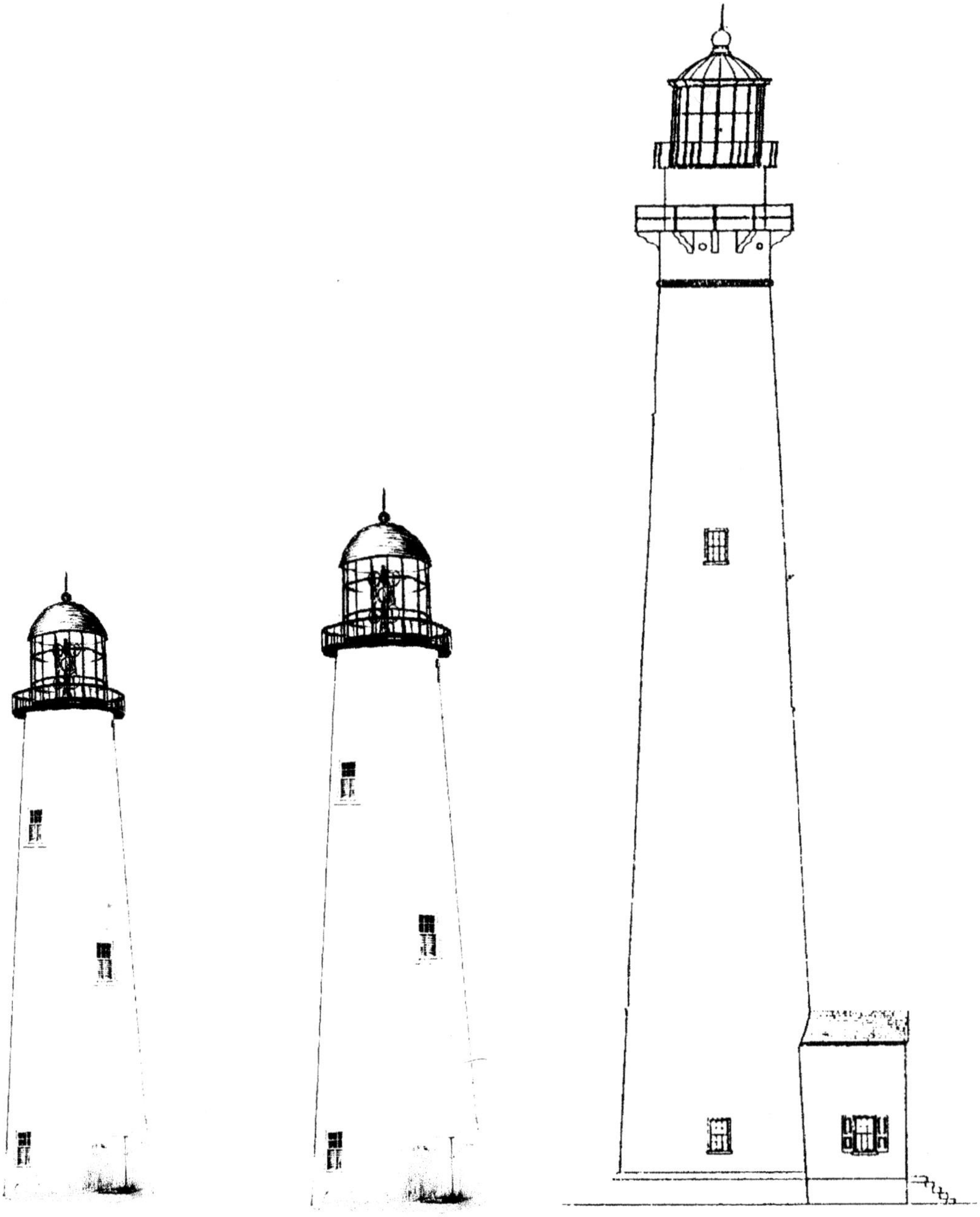

1823	1847	1859
68'	78'	145'

Lighthouses of Cape May

*"Oh! Dream of joy!
Is this indeed
the lighthouse top I see?"*

- Samuel T. Coleridge,
"Rime of the Ancient Mariner"

Behold the Cape May Lighthouse. She stands there so silently and aloof that we find it difficult to fathom her age and the epochs that have swirled about her base. At her birth (1859), the era of the steamship had not quite dawned. As the first keepers trimmed her sperm whale oil lamps and polished her lens, clipper ship captains scanned Cape May for her 30-second flash. As armies clashed at Gettysburg (1863), her beacon probed the Delaware Bay once every 30-seconds. As Queen Victoria gripped the helm of the British Empire (1837-1901), this beacon swept the sea as steadily as the rhythms of time. As the heart of Cape May City burned (1878) and entire blocks of grand hotels, shops and homes fell into heaps of blackened rubble, her light flashed behind the smoke and the flames once every thirty seconds. Every night, through great wars and great storms, through hot sunny summers and cold dark winters, her keepers carried oil up these same 217 steps and faithfully lighted the lamp. She flashed her signal every 30-seconds. Yet, she is not the first to stand here on this spit of land.

Since 1823, we know of three different lighthouses that have commanded the Jersey Cape. Have other unknown sentinels stood and then fallen before them? That very question has fascinated Cape May Lighthouse enthusiasts for years.

Photo: Corey Gilbert, TidesofTime.com, ©2000

Lighthouses of Cape May

Before 1823

On June 18, 1790, Alexander Hamilton, Secretary of the Treasury, presented the first official report on the nation's lighthouses to President Washington. His report lists all known lighthouses in the country, state by state.

Hamilton gathered his information by interviewing representatives from each of the states in the report. He lists the Sandy Hook, New Jersey Lighthouse under the state of New York, as the Wardens of the Port of New York had responsibility for its maintenance and upkeep. He lists the Cape Henlopen (Delaware) Lighthouse and "several buoys, beacons, and piers, for the security of the navigation on the Bay and River Delaware" under the state of Pennsylvania since the Philadelphia Board of Port Wardens had responsibility for those navigational aids. Consequently, Delaware received the same report as New Jersey, "There is no lighthouse nor other establishment of this nature, those on the Bay and River Delaware answering for that State."[2] Perhaps he was right about New Jersey; perhaps not.

We do have considerable evidence (though none of it official) that earlier lights have indeed marked this peninsula. Consider the testimony:

The Secretary of the Treasury, having, in consequence of the act (ninth law passed by congress taking over the maintenance of the nation's lighthouses, Aug. 7, 1789) for the establishment and support of lighthouses, directed his inquiries to that object, begs leave most respectfully to submit the result to the President of the United States of America... New Jersey - There is no known lighthouse, nor any establishment of that nature.

1 Philadelphia has always been an important seaport, accessible only through the Delaware Bay. Thus, the bay has always been a heavily traveled waterway. Merchants, military, fishermen and whalers have sailed the Delaware since well before the Revolution (Philadelphia was the nation's first capital). Cape May marks the northernmost seaward entrance to the bay. Shipping bound from England, New York City and Boston must navigate around Cape May to enter the bay. Bay pilots, ship builders, and whalers originally settled Cape May. In fact, Cape May's whaling industry in the 1600s rivaled that of Cape Cod. It doesn't seem possible that all of these seamen found safe harbor here for some 200 years (1600-1823) without some large marker or light.

2. Maps from as early as 1744 show a light marker on Cape May.

3. In 1776, colonial Philadelphia businessmen financed and constructed the seventh lighthouse to be built in the Colonies at the south entrance to the bay, Cape Henlopen.[3] Why did they not build one on Cape May? Could it be that someone had already built a lighthouse on Cape May?

4. In 1785, the Pennsylvania Board of Port Wardens purchased a tract of land on Cape May from "one Thomas Hand 2nd, Gentleman, for the purpose of erecting a beacon thereon for the benefit of navigation."[4] The site for this lighthouse is believed to be on a high bluff in front of the present location of Congress Hall.

5. The July 1801 edition of the Philadelphia Aurora contains an advertisement titled, "Seashore Entertainment At Cape May." The copy rolls on with tempting descriptions of the accommodations, food, liquors and the care of horses available to the Cape May visitor; followed by this remarkable passage: "The situation is beautiful, just on the confluence of Delaware Bay with the ocean, in sight of the Lighthouse, and affords a view of the shipping which enters and leaves the Delaware Bay…"

# *Lighthouses of Cape May*

The Cape May Lighthouse postcard rendered just after the turn of the 20th century.

6. According to the Hand family genealogy, "Japhet Hand (d: 1895) was born in a lighthouse at Cape May, New Jersey."[5] in 1815 or 17.

Was Cape May dark until 1823? It really doesn't seem so, but no one living today knows for sure. If earlier towers did mark this cape, wars and the pounding surf have hidden their legacies in the foggy mists of the cape's early history. We do know that during the Revolution, the British burned and destroyed many American lighthouses to confound American shipping. They burned Cape Henlopen "nearly to the ground."[6] If there had been a lighthouse on Cape May they would certainly have destroyed it the same way, perhaps completely. But, without a trace?

Let's consider what we do know!

The Cape Henlopen Lighthouse. If the British had built a lighthouse on Cape May, it probably would have resembled Henlopen.

1823 Lighthouse

On May 7, 1822, Congress appropriated $5,000 to "contract for the building of a lighthouse on Cape May." On July 15th, the government paid Mr. and Mrs. John Stites $300 for one acre of unstable sand upon which to build a lighthouse.[7] On March 3, 1823, Congress appropriated another $5,750 for "completing the lighthouse on Cape May."[8]

The following October, Cape May's first known lighthouse began flashing its signal out to sea. Its lantern stood 88 feet above the ocean, atop a 68 foot tall brick tower. The light had "15 lamps with 16-inch reflectors. Revolving. Removed and rebuilt in 1847, 400 yards N.E. from old site."[9] Its brick tower had a 25-foot diameter at the base and stood on a stone foundation. Its wall measured a full 6-feet thick at the bottom and 2½-feet thick at the top.[10]

Lighthouses of Cape May

Fig. 2 The first known lighthouse at Cape May 1823-1847 From Scheyichbi and the Strand, Edward S. Wheeler, 1876.

Erosion has always threatened lighthouses, especially where they have been built upon sand. Since we have no granite cliffs in Cape May, this lighthouse, by necessity, stood on shifting sands. Soon, with every high tide, the relentless pounding surf surrounded the tower and began washing away its foundation. The government discontinued its light on May 1, 1847[11], dismantled the tower, and moved it to higher ground. The location of the old lighthouse is now itself at sea, over 100 yards off shore southwest of the present tower. It lasted only 24 years.

1847 Lighthouse

As the site of the first tower surrendered to the unpredictable demands of the sea, local contractors, Samuel and Nathan Middleton were busy rebuilding it at its new location 400 yards (that's the distance of four football fields) to the northeast, safely inland from the eroding coastline.

Fig. 3 Cut off base in use, 1938. Photo courtesy of Mid-Atlantic Center for the Arts (MAC).

The new tower stood 78 feet tall. We have no known pictures, good illustrations, or further descriptions of these early lighthouses. However, from photographs of the cutoff base (Figure 3) we can see that they had a 20-25 foot diameter. If I draw those dimensions to scale and project the angles of the cutoff base to a point 68 feet above, the beautifully proportioned lighthouse in Fig. 4 appears (of course the design of the lantern and the locations of the windows is speculation based on other lighthouses of the period).

The Middletons built a round tower of red bricks resting on a stone foundation, resembling other lighthouses of its period. Though similar to its current sister, it had a shorter tower with an entry door at the base and no vestibule, painted with whitewash inside and out. A wooden stairway spiraled up the inside of the tower into a black cast iron lantern. The lantern itself was small, cramped for room, and poorly ventilated. It

Fig. 4 Author's conception of the 1847 Cape May Lighthouse.

15

Lighthouses of Cape May

contained a catoptric device that used polished mirrors to reflect and intensify the light. This device had 15 reflectors on three faces (five on each face), ten of them were 15-inch bowl shaped reflectors, and five of them were 14-inch spherical shaped reflectors. The light revolved once every three minutes. Its three faces caused it to flash once every minute.[12] Figure 5 shows a similar catoptric device that has only three bowl shaped reflectors on each face.

The 1847 lighthouse would have been quite adequate had they built it half a century earlier, but the increasing demands of Atlantic coastal shipping in the mid-1800s required more. Ships' masters began to criticize the Lighthouse Service. Wrecks became increasingly commonplace up and down the seaboard. Something had to be done!

In 1851, after being bludgeoned by volleys of complaints about the lighthouse establishment, Congress appointed a board to investigate and inspect the nation's lighthouses. The inspectors found that under the Treasury Department's Fifth Auditor, Stephen Pleasonton, the Lighthouse Service had deteriorated to a dangerous level. (See Appendix B Administration of the Fifth Auditor.) Their findings changed the lighthouse service forever. After the investigating board published its report in 1852, Congress immediately appointed a Lighthouse Board with the charge of totally reorganizing the system.

Cape May's inspection, dated June 25, 1851 (see Appendix C for the complete report), found the station to be in a sad state of repair. The tower had been "rough and rudely built," leaking, unpainted and rusty. The light revolved irregularly and lacked ventilation. The keeper had no training, no printed instructions, and a poor state of morale. He lacked basic supplies such as paint, trimming scissors, brooms, and brushes. His quarters leaked, its plaster was cracked and many of its windows were broken. The lifesaving boathouse was locked up tight and the keeper didn't have a key.

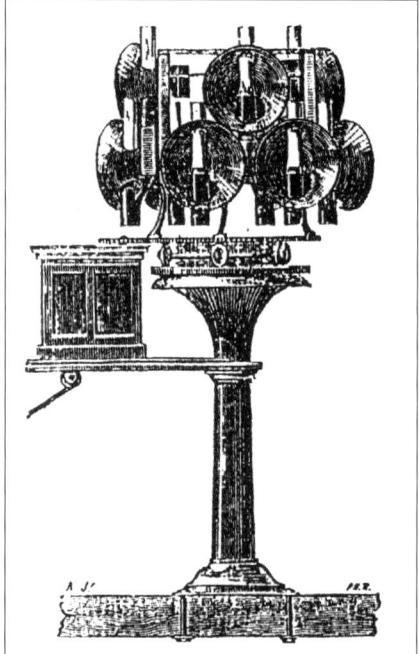
Fig. 5 Revolving Catoptric Light.

In short, the station received the kind of report card that causes youngsters to dawdle on their way home from school hoping to delay the inevitable confrontation.

Further, the unceasing pounding of technology had swamped lighthouse number two. Specifically, its old fashioned catoptric reflectors couldn't hold a candle to the new first-order Fresnel lens, the most powerful lens to this day for seacoast lights. The "inevitable confrontation" loomed. The newly appointed Lighthouse Board's report (dated January 30, 1852) calls for the upgrading of nine important seacoast lights:

Fig. 6 The last pieces of the 1847 lighthouse waiting on the beach for the sea to reclaim its remains. Photo courtesy of Robert Fite.

```
... Second only in importance to the foregoing proposed new
structures is the necessity for substituting first-order lens
apparatus in place of the present inferior reflectors, and
giving to each tower an elevation of not less than 150 feet,
at the following points, where first-class sea-coast lights are
indispensable to the safety of commerce...
```

Needless to say, Cape May's "rough," short (78-foot) tower with its "inferior reflectors" and bad report card made it onto the list of nine. The other lucky sites were: Cape Henlopen, Cape Charles, Cape Henry, Cape Hatteras, Cape Lookout, Cape Fear, Cape Romain, and Morris Island, (Charleston) S.C.

On March 3, 1857, Congress appropriated $40,000 "For rebuilding and fitting with firstorder apparatus the lighthouse at Cape May entrance to the Delaware Bay."[13] That appropriation fired the final broadside into the 10-year old lighthouse. And, as we will see, for

Lighthouses of Cape May

Cape May it couldn't have happened at a better time!

The board left the second lighthouse standing after the new lighthouse had begun operation, but demolished it in 1862. "The old light tower...having been found to be productive of danger, by misleading mariners by day, has been thrown down, and steps taken to dispose of the old materials."[14] Those steps were to sell the bricks. Keeper Downes E. Foster kept a record of who bought the bricks and how many bricks were sold. About 70 buyers bought loads of cleaned bricks for $3.00 per thousand, and quantities of "brickbats" (bricks still cemented together) for $.50 per load.[15] All of the sales totaled $150. Many Cape May County homes and chimneys contain bricks from this early lighthouse.

They saved about eight feet of the base, roofed it over and used it for storage as a spring house (Figure 3). Its location is approximately 420-feet toward the ocean from the new tower, like its predecesssor, also at sea, but just beyond the present (2000) low water line.

1859 Lighthouse

Most days you get up in the morning feeling terrific. You know you're about to have a great day, and everything you do goes just right. We all need days like this to keep us going. Well, the nation's lighthouses hadn't seen very many good days before the 1850s, but that was about to change! Congress had found the Fifth Auditor's tight budgeting of the lighthouse system (See Appendix B) to have been catastrophic. Money had begun to flow seaward from Washington. The new Lighthouse Board, comprised of marine-savvy people, controlled the purse strings. Fresnel had perfected his lenses and Congress had ordered his first order lens for all important seacoast lighthouses. Commander Matthew C. Perry brought the first two lenses from France into the U.S. for the Twin Lights at Navesink, New Jersey in 1840. The science and technology of the lighthouse

1859 Lighthouse site as originally built with two cottages. Photo courtesy of MAC.

19

Lighthouses of Cape May

Captain George G. Meade

(pharology) had reached a pinnacle. And, that's just when the Army Engineers rolled into Cape May in 1857 with $40,000 to build the state-of-the-art sentinel that now stands at the north entrance to the Delaware Bay.

Sadly, we have found no evidence to support the folklore that one of those engineers was George Gordon Meade, the great Civil War general that led the Army of the Potomac into their victorious battle at Gettysburg. (Interestingly, both generals in that battle, Meade and Lee, were formerly peaceful Army engineers transformed by the war into combat generals.) However, it seems that every salty old Cape Islander that you ask will try to convince you that Meade was one of the builders.

But Meade is very probably the architect of the Cape May Lighthouse. The examination of Meade's similar known lighthouse designs (Absecon, Barnegat, Jupiter Inlet), leaves very little doubt that he designed this one. In 1852, the Army Corps of Engineers assigned young second lieutenant Meade to "engineering duties" in the Delaware Bay. In 1855, Meade inspected the old Barnegat Lighthouse and made recommendations for its replacement. He commanded the 4th and 7th Lighthouse Districts (the 4th includes South Jersey, Delaware, Maryland, and the Delaware Bay) from April 13, 1854 to May 31, 1856 when Lt. William F. Raynolds relieved him. At the time of the change of command, they were building the Absecon Lighthouse, finishing it in 1857. While the Army Corps was in Cape May, Capt. Meade was surveying the Great Lakes (1856-1861).[16]

Many times the Corps assigned the young lieutenant to survey and inspect sites where they planned to build new or replacement lights. Could he have performed that duty for this lighthouse? Perhaps. But,

20

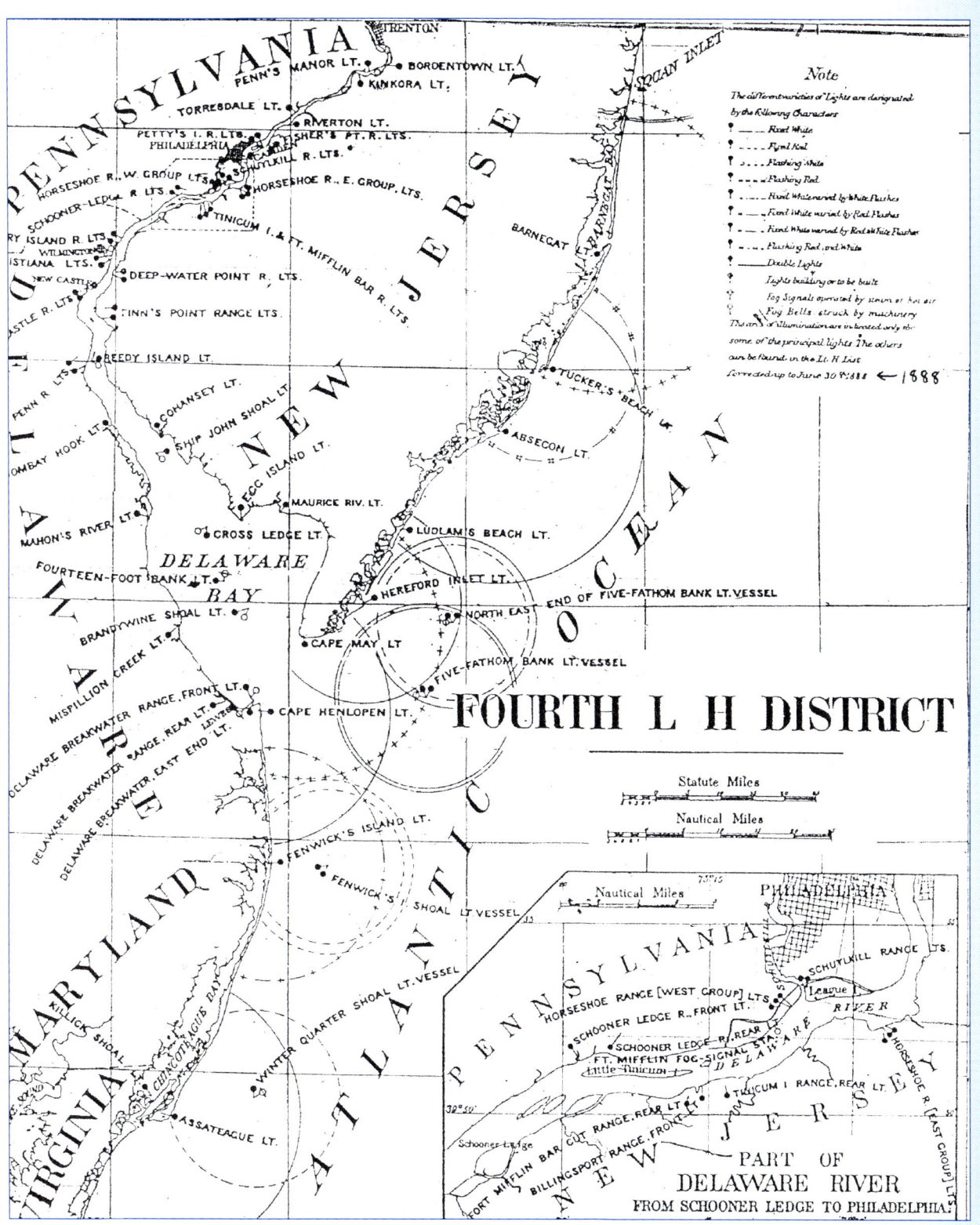

Fig. 7: Fourth Lighthouse District (1888)

Lighthouses of Cape May

Lt. George G. Meade was not a member of the engineers attached to this Lighthouse District at the time of the construction of this tower. The following is from an official log entry, Fourth District Engineers:

> "The present tower and buildings were erected by mechanics and laborers employed and paid in part by day and in part by the month; commenced under the direction of Captain (now Lieutenant Colonel) William F. Raynolds, continued by Captain W.B. Franklin, and finished by the late Major (Hartman) Bache, all of the Corps of Engineers, U.S.A. Tower finished 1859; dwellings finished in 1860."

They did build a magnificent lighthouse! It soars into the sky 157 feet, 6 inches from the ground to the ventilator ball on top of the lantern. It is a graceful yet staunchly solid structure, possessing the unlikely characteristics of both a ballet dancer and a Sumo wrestler.

The first keeper of the new lighthouse, Wm. C. Gregory, climbed the stairs and lighted the lamp for the first time at sunset on Halloween Eve, October 31, 1859. For you astrology buffs, that makes the Cape May Lighthouse a Scorpio. Scorpio is a fixed watery sign, energetic, independent, passionate, determined. It is the sign of a governor or inspector. Its color is deep red. Scorpio's harmonious signs for business or companionship are Cancer (the crab) and Pisces (the fish). Sounds to me like the Cape May Lighthouse is a solid Scorpio.

Today, the Cape May Lighthouse is the second oldest continually operating lighthouse in the country, after the Sandy Hook, New Jersey lighthouse (1764) which still guides shipping into New York harbor. (Although it stood dark during World War II, as the military extinguished all lighthouses during the war.)

In the next chapter, we will take a close look at the lighthouse "finished 1859," exploring its features in detail from the ground up, just the way the Engineers built it.

A TOUR OF THE LIGHTHOUSE

*"Cicero was not so eloquent as thou,
thou nameless column with the buried base"*
- Byron

The late Ada Palmer, daughter of keeper Harry Palmer, at the double doors of entrance to the vestibule.
Photo courtesy of the Palmer family.

The most plausible theory on the construction of the tower holds that the builders constructed the spiral stairway as they laid the brickwork. (We surmise this because they pinned the leaves of the stairway into the masonry.) They actually worked on the inner wall from the stairway itself carrying bricks and mortar up these same steps. They worked on the outer wall using scaffolding erected outside the tower. One thing is certain; the builders were master masons. The alternating mortar lines, inside and outside, follow a perfectly straight sight line up from the

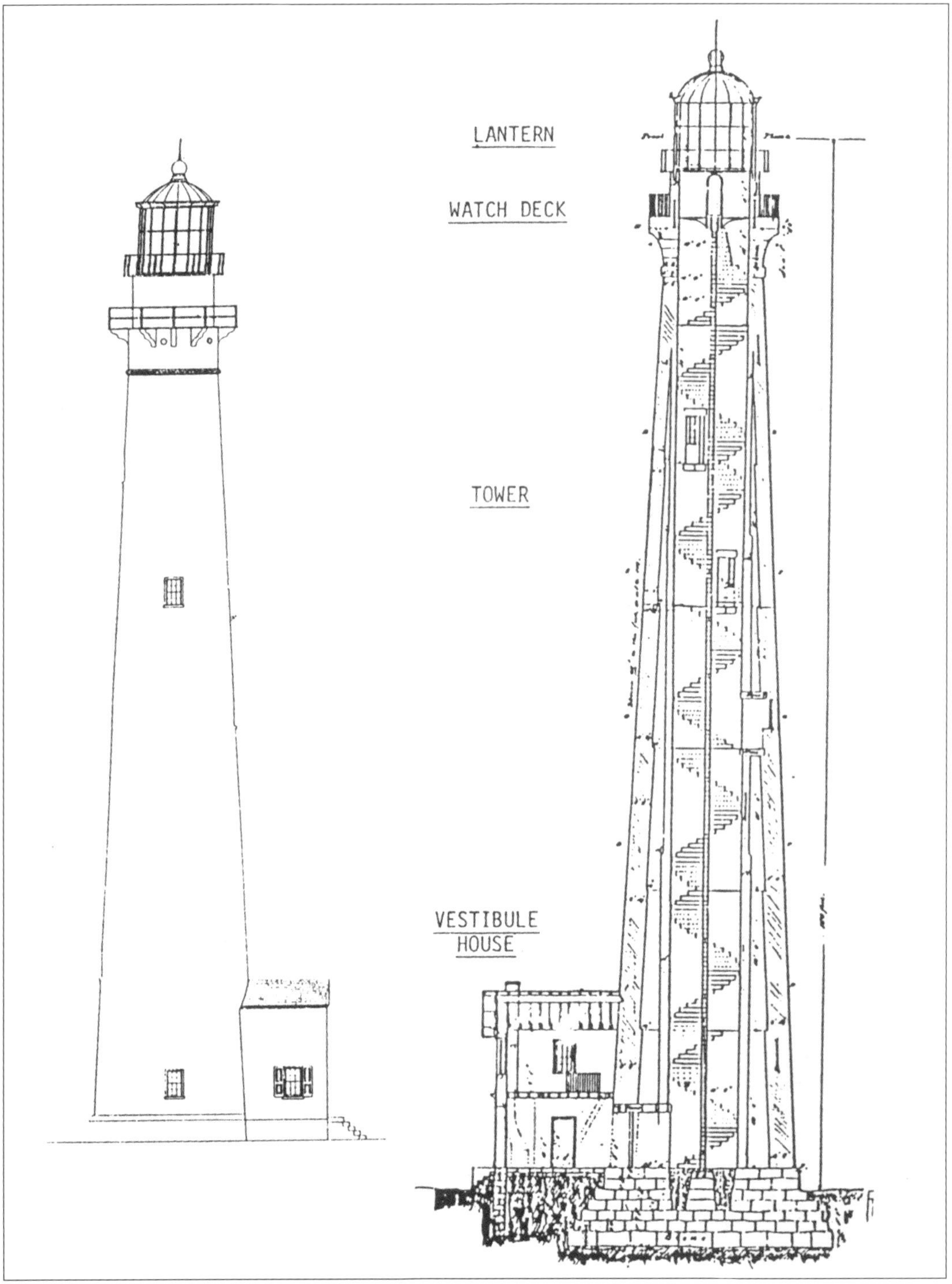
LANTERN
WATCH DECK
TOWER
VESTIBULE HOUSE

Outside and cutaway diagrams of the Cape May Lighthouse. Illustration courtesy of MAC.

base to the watch room. Each of the courses lays impeccably level and true. A reinforcing stratum of bricks laid crosswise, so that you can see only the ends of the bricks, separates every five courses. The bricks themselves have curves that follow the curvature of the walls inside and out. Present day master masons who visit the lighthouse marvel at the beautiful arches on the ground floor, the detailing throughout, the smooth corner mitres, and the workmen's obvious pride in craftsmanship.

To visit the watch room at the top, you must climb 205 steps. Five concrete steps outside the entrance lead you onto a short porch with one more step up into the vestibule. When you have passed through the vestibule and into the tower, the spiral stairway confronts you with its circular ascent of 198 iron "leaves" from its base to the watch room. When you make that one more step from the iron stairway up into the watch room (for a total of 199), you will see 12 more wooden steps leading up into the lantern. So, to tend the light, the keepers of old climbed a total of 217 steps every watch, carrying loads of varying weights that included oil, fire, wicks, cleaning supplies, whatever they needed to carry out their daily duties. No wonder the ladies admired the keepers; they did have a reputation for being in great shape.

Vestibule

A two-story vestibule with double doors forms the entrance to the tower. Its doors open into a hallway with oil storage rooms on each side. Before 1893, when the use of kerosene forced the storage of oil outside of the tower, these rooms contained bulk oil tanks. From these rooms the keepers filled their oil containers, lighted a miniature Aladdin's-type lamp, called a lucerne, and carried the oil and flame up to the lantern. The second floor served as a storage room for miscellaneous supplies, accessed by a ladder through the ceiling

A Tour of the Lighthouse

of the oil room on the right. Oddly, this is an inconvenient solution for accessing such an important storage area. If you ever visit the Barnegat Lighthouse, probably designed by the same architect and built almost simultaneously with the Cape May Lighthouse (1857-1859), you will see a completely different solution: you can walk from the second landing in the tower onto the second floor of Barnegat's vestibule through a spacious doorway!

Tower

The lighthouse tower stands 145 feet tall on 12 feet of subterranean stone blocks. This subterranean foundation spreads out pyramid-like, giving the lighthouse a much broader footprint than you can see. Several courses of these blocks are visible above ground.

Double Walls

Like ancient castle ramparts, the tower has double walls, an inner wall and an outer wall. These two brick masonry walls give the tower unbelievable strength and the ability to withstand whatever the elements may throw at it, such as a wind five times greater than the fiercest hurricane that the North Atlantic can produce.

The outer wall has a conical shape, like a gigantic upside down ice cream cone, with an outside diameter of 27 feet at the bottom narrowing by exactly half to 13 feet 6 inches at the top. The masonry on the outer wall alone is 3 feet 9 inches thick at the bottom and 1 foot 6 inches thick at the top.

The inner wall is a straight cylinder, a brick tube 9 inches thick for its entire length with an inside diameter of 10 feet 6 inches all the way up from the bottom to just below the watch room where the inner and outer walls converge.

Beautiful arches connect the two walls at the ground floor and at each window. The ground floor arches support the base of the inner wall and relieve its weight. All of the arches and the empty air space between the walls reduce the overall weight of the lighthouse without sacrificing any strength.

Spiral Stairway

The inner wall supports a breathtaking cast iron spiral stairway of 198 leaves. Thirty steps separate each of its six landings, and twelve more steps lead from the last landing up to the watch room (180 steps + 6 landings + 12 steps up into the watch room = 198). Every landing faces a different direction (90°), making a quarter turn from the landing above and below it. The arched brick ceiling, known as "barrel vaulting," above the window at each landing gives additional support to the tower. Small square holes on both sides of the window arches allow circulation of air between the two walls and prevent moisture accumulation.

Fig. 9: Spiral stairway. Photo by John Bailey.

Each step and landing is an individually cast "leaf." These leaves stack one on top of another up the center column. Pins on the outer edge of each leaf and landing connect the stairway solidly to the inner wall. The architect chose cast iron because it is fire proof, and the open iron work allows sound, light, and air to travel freely throughout the tower.

In 1865, they added the outer railing, probably at the request of the keepers. (Until then the stairs had no hand railing.) The railing too is cast iron with decorative spirals at the ends (see Fig 10).

The last landing from the top, just below the watch room, is smaller than the others and has no window. Round portholes illuminate this area. The rough grey panels between the portholes are the

A Tour of the Lighthouse

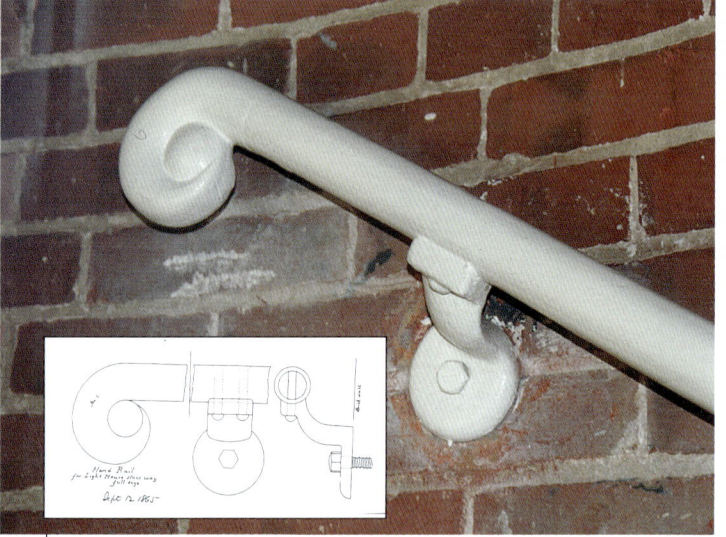

Fig. 10: Decorative railing details (original designer's drawing and as executed). Illustration courtesy of MAC. Photo by John Bailey.

butt ends of the granite brackets that support the watch room's gallery. The ceiling above this landing is beneath the floor of the watch room. The guide pulley for the weight that drove the original lens still hangs from this ceiling in its original location. The hole in the wall directly across from the pulley is at the top of the drop tube. This is where the weight that drove the Fresnel lens slowly descended to the tube's outlet in the barrel vaulting at the topmost window (Fig 11).

Watch Room

At the top of the tower just below the lantern is the watch room. This is where the keepers stood their watches and observed the light. The room has the feeling of a smart old tug boat bridge with its tongue and groove flooring, light varnished wainscoting walls, and polished bronze air vents. A wooden stairway with twelve steps curves along the wall and leads up into the lantern. A beautifully detailed iron door (Fig. 14) with a solid brass knob opens onto the outside gallery. Ten huge granite brackets each five feet long support the gallery.

In 1998, during the restoration of the watch room floor, workers were removing the old planks when they were surprised to discover a radial tongue and groove floor beneath. (Fig 12). Although, this hidden floor was obviously original and an architectural work of art, its condition was so poor that current funding couldn't pay for its restoration. The architect ordered it carefully covered by the restored flooring for future generations to one day uncover.

The keepers spent their nightly 4-hour watches in this room, ensuring that the light burned brightly and never missed its 30-second flash. During their watches the keepers rewound the clockwork mechanism, trimmed the wick when required, and maintained the oil level in the lamp. They lighted the lamp one-half hour before sunset and extinguished it one-half hour after sunrise. They always kept the lamp lighted during limited visibility weather. During their long lonely vigils, the keepers busied themselves by dusting the inside of the lantern, sweeping the stairs, and keeping everything tidy and shipshape. The curved service closet in this room contained all of the supplies they needed to perform their duties.

Fig. 11: Drop tube outlet at the topmost window. Photo by John Bailey

Telephone System

A telephone system "with magneto call bell" connected the watch room with each of the keepers' dwellings. The keepers used this system to wake their watch relief and for any communication needs between the lofty watch room and the ground.

One stormy night, on June 12, 1891, lightning struck the ball on the roof, streaked down the metal framework of the lantern, leaped from the pedestal of the lamp to the iron of the watch room, passed around the iron gallery to the lightning rod, and followed the electric call bell wires into the keepers' dwellings causing "much damage to the interiors."[17] They didn't report any injuries, but one can well imagine the topic of conversation around the cottages for some time!

Fig. 12: Radial flooring uncovered during restoration of the watch room. Photo courtesy of Watson & Henry Architects.

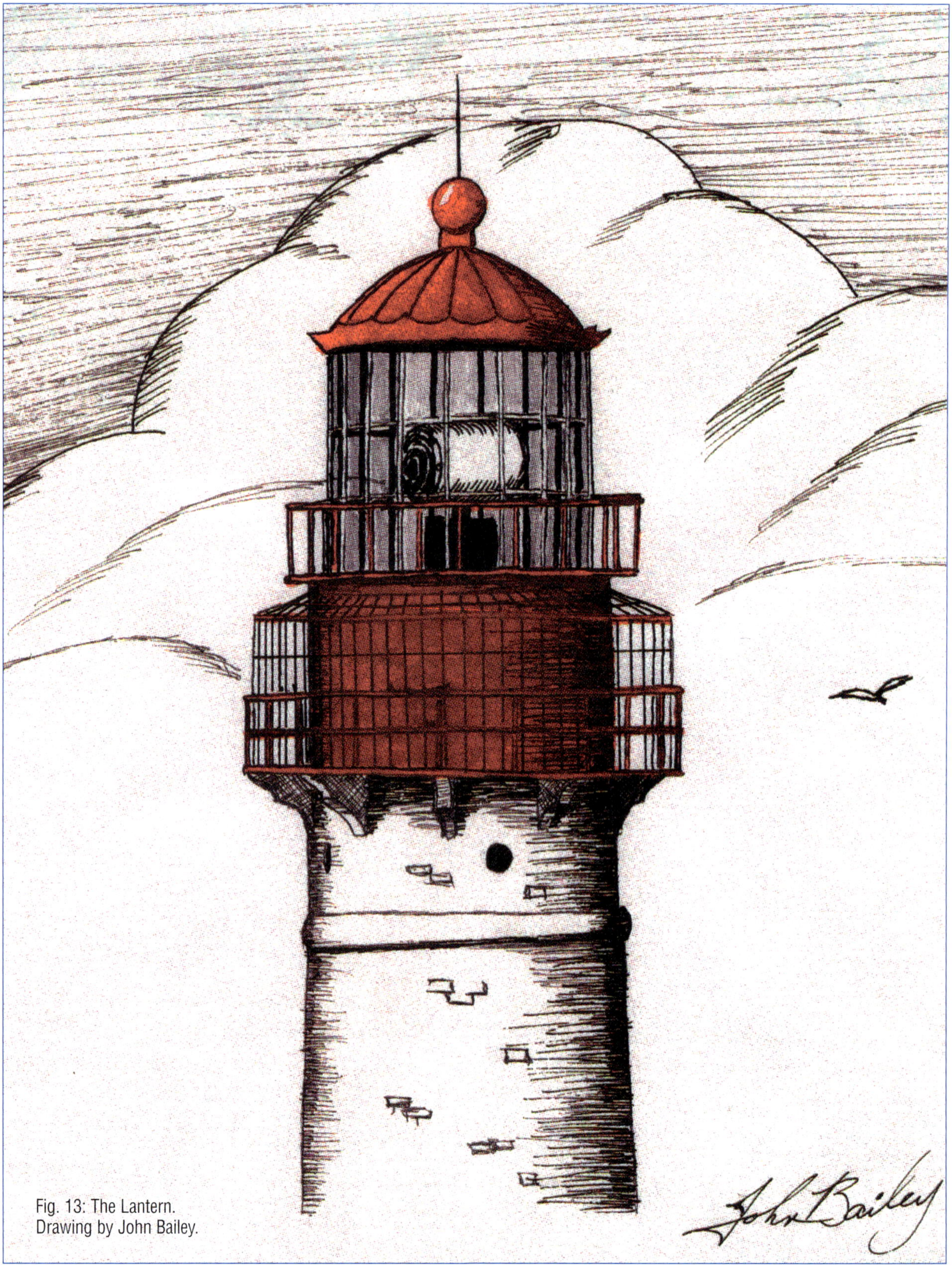
John Bailey

Fig. 13: The Lantern.
Drawing by John Bailey.

Fig. 14: Original lens' pedestal. Photo by John Bailey.

Watch room door leading to the exterior walkway
Photo by John Bailey

Lantern

At the very top of the brick tower stands the lantern, the roofed-over room surrounded with windows, that crowns lighthouses everywhere. The lantern is the very reason the lighthouse exists. The lantern houses, protects and displays the light.

The lantern that tops the Cape May Lighthouse stands 12 feet 6 inches tall with a diameter of approximately 12 feet. It has 16 faces of windows, one for each of the flash panels on its original Fresnel lens (see Fig. 17). The builders used cast or wrought iron for its railings, posts, circular floor, and roof joists; bronze for all of the sash

31

# A Tour of the Lighthouse

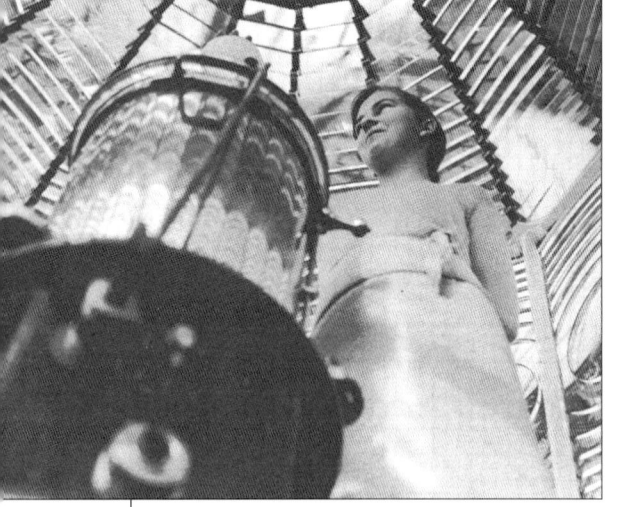

Fig. 15: Ada Palmer inside the lens, with her hand on the new experimental electric lamp, 1933. Photo courtesy of the Palmer family.

bars, sills, lintels, and glass stops; and, copper for the gracefully domed roof and ventilator ball.

Ventilation in a flame-illuminated lantern is critical. Without proper ventilation, the lamp would not burn brightly; smoke, soot, and fumes would accumulate inside the lantern, further diminishing the intensity of the light and making it difficult for the keepers to work inside. Five 8-inch registers in the watch room feed this lantern's ventilator ball. These registers control the proper air flow throughout the lantern. In Figure 14, you can see these registers in the watch room wall.

Originally wire mesh netting surrounded the outside of the lantern windows to protect them from the wild birds that proliferate at Cape May Point during the peak migratory periods. Without protective netting, heavy birds, such as ducks and geese would become confused by the light, crash through the windows and possibly damage the apparatus. So many fly into the light during storms that Ada Palmer, the last keeper's daughter, earned her spending money collecting the bodies of crashed birds for Roger Tory Peterson. Peterson, the famous author and ornithologist, used the bodies for detail studies of their markings and coloring for his birding books. The 1994 restoration project replaced the glass in the lantern with thick safety glass which eliminated the need for the protective netting. This gave the lantern a new cleaner profile.

During daylight hours, the lens itself had to be protected from the ultraviolet rays of direct sunlight. In the same way one can start a fire by focusing the sun's light through a magnifying glass. the prisms in the lens could also magnify the sun's rays causing a fire. The lantern contained eight roller curtains, which the keepers pulled down at sunrise. These curtains covered the lantern's windows shielding the lens.

Fresnel Lens

The original exquisite First-Order, revolving Fresnel Lens virtually filled this lantern. Henry LaPaute fabricated the lens in Paris and shipped it here.

The inventor of the lens, Augustin Fresnel (pronounced Fray-nel), 1788-1827, a French physicist, made several important discoveries in light wave theory and applied his theorems to lighthouse technology. He perfected his lens in 1822, and to this day nothing has surpassed it in efficiency. Fresnel's First-Order lens resembles a giant beehive of prisms girdled about the middle by a smooth magnifying lens (for fixed lights) or by a series of bullseye magnifying lenses (called flash panels) for flashing lights like Cape May (See Figures 16 and 17). Reflecting and refracting (catadioptric) prisms above and below the flash panels actually bend all spreading light rays that try to escape the flash panels themselves back into a horizontal focused beam, parallel with that of the flash panels. Each of the 16 sides hurls a bright narrow beam of light over twenty miles across the ocean. With a good interior lamp, only the horizon or height of the lens could limit its range (See Appendix A, Cape May Lighthouse at a Glance, Geography, Geographical Range).

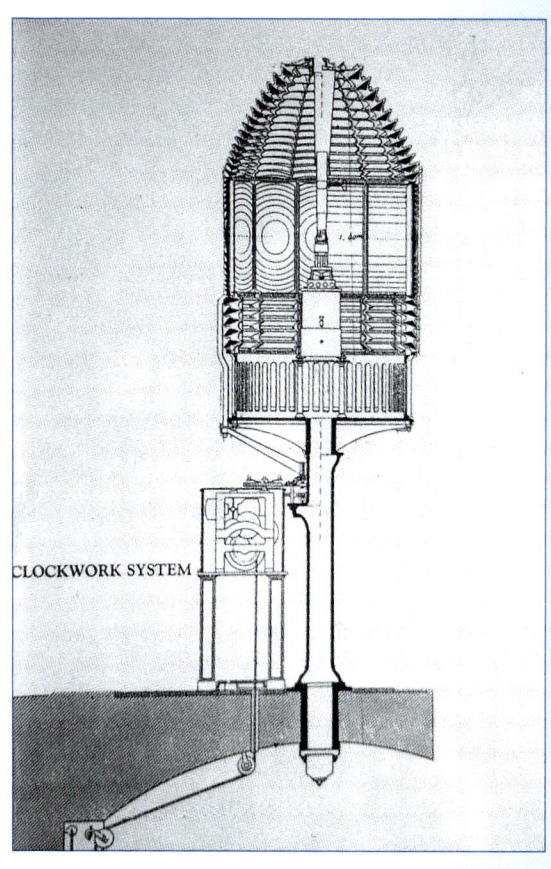

Fig. 16: Revolving Fresnel lens. Flash panels on the left side, smooth lens on right side. Illustration courtesy of MAC.

The size of a lens determines its order and use. First-Order is the largest. Used for seacoast lights, they stand 7 feet 10 inches tall with a six-foot diameter. The keepers actually went inside of them to service their lamps. Sixth-Order lenses are the smallest. Used within harbors, they stand 3 feet tall with a diameter just large enough to contain a small lamp.

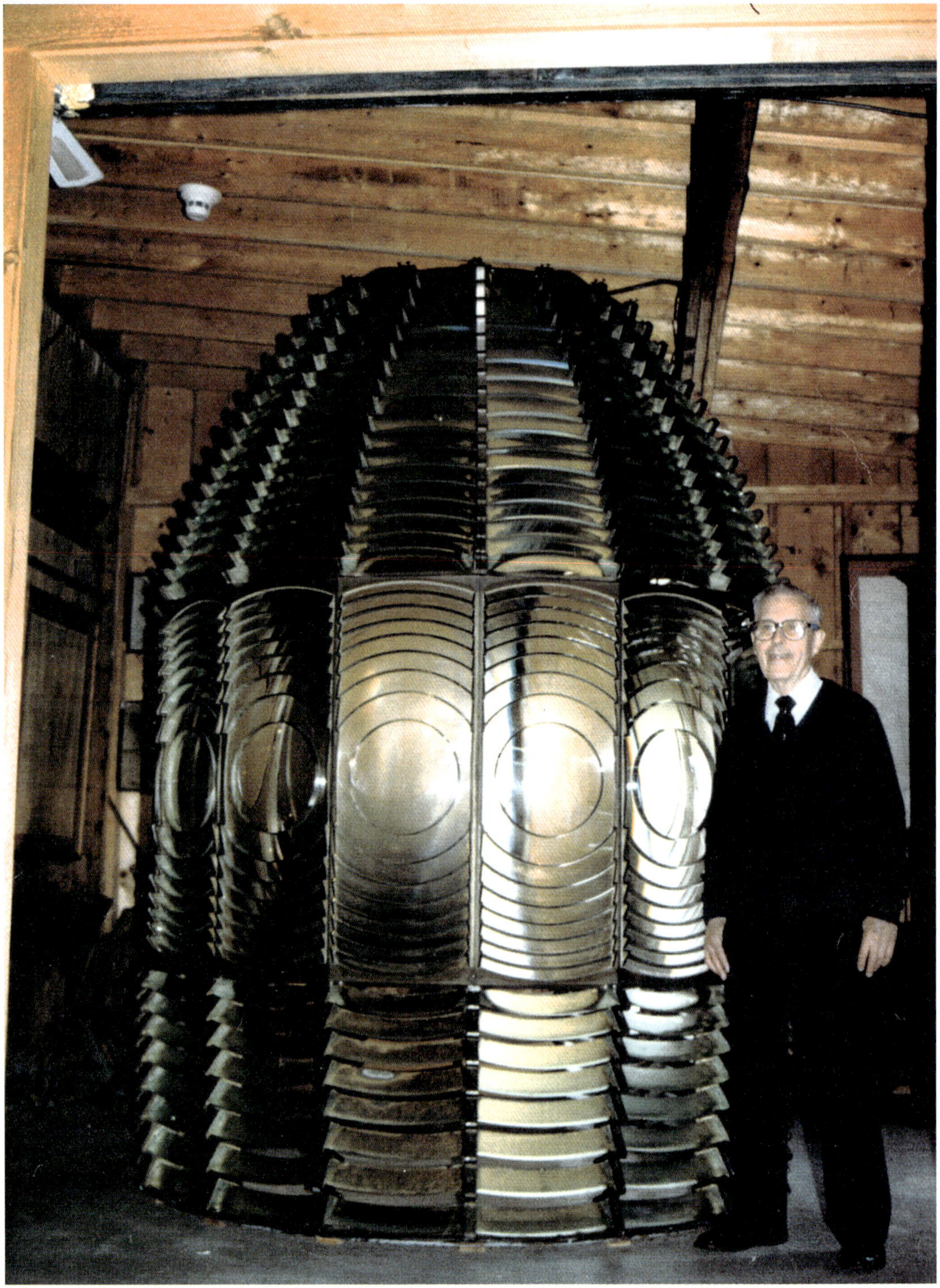

Fig. 17: Cape May's First-Order lens with MAC keeper (Lighthouse guide) Charles Rumsey. Photo courtesy of MAC.

The revolving First-Order Fresnel lens with flash panels revolves around the lamp; the passing panels provide the flashes. The speed of revolution, controlled by a centrifugal governor, determines the frequency of the flash.

This lantern's First-Order lens, now on display at the Cape May County Historical Museum[18] in Cape May Court House (see Fig. 17), revolved once every 8 minutes around a fixed lamp. Sixteen flash panels caused it to flash every 30 seconds at every point around it. The lens rode on a "chariot" that had 10 wheels and 20 guide wheels. A clockwork weight system, which works like the weights that drive grandfather or cuckoo clocks, drove the lens.

As the great lens slowly revolved, the weight gradually descended on a long cable, 28 feet from the clockwork at the base of the lens to the bottom of the drop tube located between the inner and outer walls. To rewind the mechanism, the keepers needed simply to wind the weight back to the top and let it descend again. The entire system consumed no outside energy and worked with little effort (we need to bring that kind of thinking back into our world). The long cable allowed the mechanism to run 8 hours on a single rewind.

Lamps

The first known device to illuminate this lighthouse consisted of "three hydraulic lamps."[19] They were probably the 5-wick, hydraulic float lamps that George G. Meade designed around 1853, as the Lighthouse Service had adopted and used these lamps extensively for First-Order Fresnel lenses at the time they built this lighthouse. Meade's lamps burned sperm whale oil.

A Funck First-Order, 5-wick, hydraulic float lamp (Fig. 18) replaced the first lamps some time after 1878 when the government converted all lighthouses to kerosene which had replaced the too expensive sperm whale oil. The Lighthouse Service used this lamp

A Tour of the Lighthouse

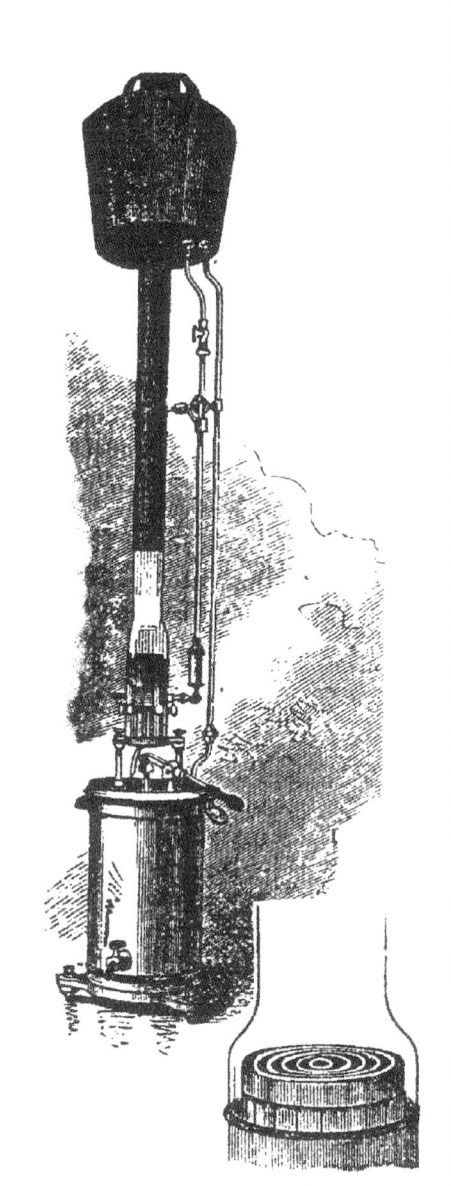

Five wick lamp for a 1st order Fresnel lens

Fig. 18: A 5-wick Funck hydraulic float lamp. Illustration courtesy of MAC.

almost exclusively in First-Order lighthouses, possibly because its inventor, Mr. Funck, worked at the Service's principal supply depot. It reigned supreme as the lamp of choice until the invention of the incandescent oil vapor lamp. When they converted this lighthouse to the incandescent oil vapor lamp in 1902, the Funck lamp that they removed had "1878" stamped into it. No one is sure exactly when this lighthouse was converted to kerosene, but the kerosene-containing oil house was built here in 1893. So, it happened sometime between 1878 and 1893.

In 1902 the new incandescent oil vapor lamp replaced the Funck lamp. The oil vapor lamp had a bright white mantle similar to those in Cape May's gas lights and Coleman's camp lanterns.

In 1933, the government removed the oil vapor lamp and electrified the Cape May Lighthouse with an experimental electric lamp. The Cape May, Delaware Bay, and Sewell's Point Railroad was running its electric trolleys across the site as early as 1903 (see Fig. 20), and most of the homes on the cape used electricity for lighting in the 1920s. However, documentation places the electrification of the light in the year 1933. The head keeper's daughter, Ada Palmer (Fig. 15) has her hand resting upon what is probably the first electric lamp. (The picture has a 1933 date.) The shiny brass tank beneath the bulb contained the oil and pump system for the previous light, the oil vapor lamp. Placing the bulb on the tank located it in the exact spot as the old lamp, on the same plane as the flash panels in the lens.

The early bulbs didn't have the intensity of the oil vapor lamp. Ada Palmer told me that, right after the electrification, she was riding home at night with her husband and they both remarked how the light seemed noticeably much weaker. However, as with the pop-up toaster and the refrigerator, electricity is so much easier to use.

The Lighthouse Service used this lantern as an experimental laboratory and tested several different electrical units here. Always, however, they conducted their experiments "with provisions being made to reduce the possibilities of extinguishment." In 1938, they installed an automatic electric lamp. These lamps had multiple bulb holders. When the service bulb burned out, a fresh one automatically moved into its place and took over. Should the power fail, an emergency generator came on line and the light barely skipped a beat. Automation thus eliminated the need for a permanently stationed keeper and marked the end of a 2,598-year era of maritime tradition.

The Current Beacon

In 1946, the Coast Guard removed the great Fresnel lens and automatic electric lamp. They placed the lens on permanent loan to the Cape May County Historical Museum. However, the lens drive mechanism has never been accounted for. After removing the Fresnel lens, they installed the present rotating beacon. Its 1,000 watt bulb, with a 36-inch Fresnel bullseye lens on each end of it, produces a beam of light that you can see for 24 miles. The beacon rotates once every 30 seconds and the two lenses cause the beam to flash at 15-second intervals, thus changing the Cape May interval from its traditional 30-second flash. Like the beacon it replaced, this lamp also has automatic bulb replacement and, until 1994, an emergency generator system. During the 1994 restoration, the Coast Guard removed the generator from its location in the oil house, deeming it no longer necessary.

This particular rotating beacon is an advanced, one-of-a-kind,

A Tour of the Lighthouse

Fig. 19: Present beacon in the lighthouse lantern. Photos by John Bailey.

experimental system that has been running perfectly since 1946. It is an historically significant beacon and predates the electrical setups in other lighthouses today. It is totally unique. When the Coast Guard installed this beacon, they were experimenting with different systems. The Cape May Lighthouse became a favorite experimental site since it was adjacent to both a major U.S. Coast Guard Base and a delightful shore resort, where officials and their families could mix business with the pleasures of sun bathing.

A TOUR OF THE GROUNDS

Fig. 20: Electric trolley at the lighthouse station, ca 1902. Charles Holmes, motorman; Morton, conductor. Note the third keeper's dwelling under construction to the right of the second cottage. Photo from the collection of H. Gerald MacDonald.

Descriptions of the lighthouse grounds in the early 1900s sound idyllic. The tall lighthouse overlooks two white clapboard cottages with red lead trim and green shutters. A whitewashed slat fence surrounds the dwellings. Red brick walkways connect the houses with the tower, the oil house, and the three frame privies. All of the buildings shimmer bright white in the sun. Off toward the ocean stands the cut-off base of the old lighthouse storage room, a brick barn, and a stable. A sandy dirt path leads from the barns to a one-and-a-half acre garden. The keeper's wife, silhouetted against rows of tall corn, is hoeing her prized Jersey tomatoes. She wipes her brow and waves to the passing trolley filled with people in straw hats and bonnets on their way from the steamboat landing to Cape May and a vacation by the sea. Beyond the grass-covered dunes, the lifesaving station bakes in the sun, its lifeboat ramp awash in the surf. Gulls and

A Tour of the Grounds

sandpipers work the edge of the sea for tiny crabs and clams. Sails dot the shimmering ocean. Ready to sign on as a lighthouse keeper? Before you do, let's take a closer look at the duties of the keeper at the turn of the last century.

ALEXANDER WHILLDIN, FOUNDER OF SEA GROVE.

Alexander Whilldin, illustration from Scheyichbi and the Strand, Edward S. Wheeler, 1876

Property

The property that the government accumulated for the Cape May station, covered about 4 acres. Most of that land has since been turned over to the state of New Jersey for the State Park and Migratory Bird Sanctuary. Congress purchased the first tract of land, about one acre (of what was then known as Stite's Beach), on July 15, 1822 from Mr. and Mrs. John Stites for $300.[20] The ocean long ago claimed that acreage. They paid $1,150 for a second tract (about two acres) bought from "Alexander Whilldin and wife" on April 9, 1847.[21] Most of that property too is now under water. The government purchased the final tract (two more acres) for this lighthouse again from Mr. and Mrs. Alexander Whilldin on April 8, 1858 for $500.[22] The Whilldins owned an extensive farm that included most of Cape May Point, portions of Lower Township, and the present state park.

The four acres had various uses and agreements. The lighthouse site, enclosed by a "board and wire fence," occupied 2.65

40

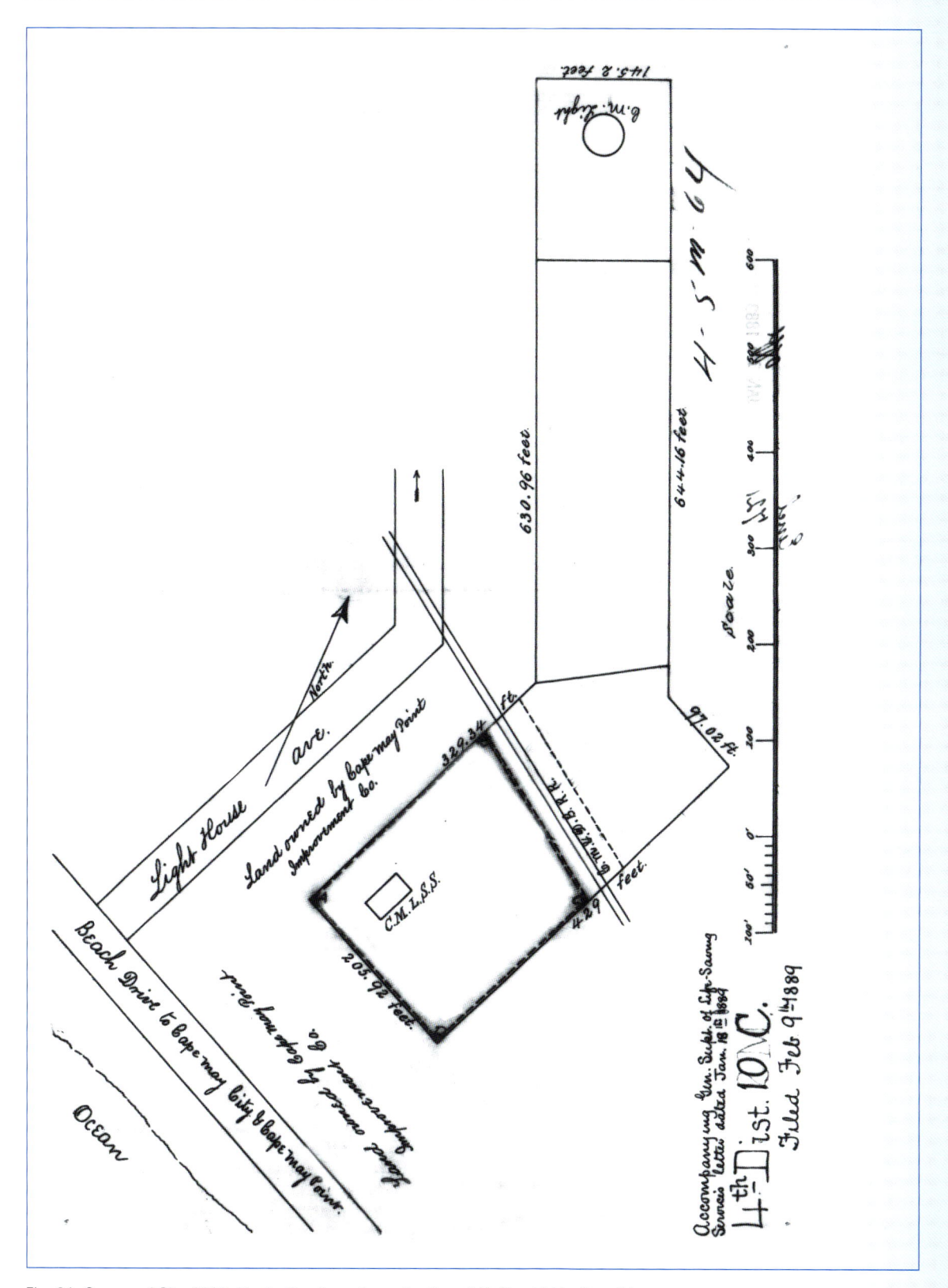

Fig. 21: Survey of Site 1889. Illustration from the collection of H. Gerald MacDonald

A Tour of the Grounds

Fig. 22: The Keepers dwellings after 1903. Photo from the collection of H. Gerald MacDonald.

acres. The Cape May, Delaware Bay, and Sewell's Point Railroad Co. had an agreement with the government to run their electric trolley across the property. Their right-of-way consumed .25 acres. The Lifesaving Station used 1.1 acres.

The lighthouse's enclosed area contained the lighthouse, barns, dwellings, and garden, much the same way in which the military fences off its bases today.

The trolley tracks passed approximately 550 feet from the tower and are now under water. In fact, the 1907 description places the high water mark "about 1100 feet "[23] (almost the length of four football fields) from the tower. The surf now occupies much of that land. The trolleys offered free transportation for officials and employees of the Lighthouse Service, who carried passes obtained at the District Engineers' Office.

The original lifesaving station had such an up-to-date modern facility that the Lifesaving Service featured its building and appli-

Fig. 23: Lifesaving service illustration page from *History of the Centennial*. Courtesy of MAC

Figure 24. The Cape May Lighthouse site, 1950s. The lifesaving station is in the foreground.
Photo from the collection of H. Gerald MacDonald.

ances as the center of their exhibit at the Centennial Exposition in Fairmount Park, Philadelphia (May - November 1876) before they moved it to this site.

No one knows of the final fate of the Centennial structure. The service built new buildings inland from the old station that survived until 1958 when the surf surrounded their foundations. The main building stood abandoned when, in the summer of 1959, fire destroyed the remains. A storm that devastated the Jersey coast in March, 1962, claimed the boat house. And the lifesaving station was gone!

Figure 24 shows the site layout. The lifesaving station, surrounded by an erosion-resisting seawall, stands in the foreground. Behind the lifesaving station, fencing encloses the barns, the

Cape May Point Light House, Cape May, N. J.
20654

Fig. 25: The final answer, sometime after 1903. Postcard was canceled on July 8, 1925

dwellings, and the tower. The round building is the base of the 1847 lighthouse tower. The trolleys ran between the fence and the lifesaving station near the dirt road.

Buildings

Keepers' Dwellings

Over the years, the service built three keepers' dwellings. Only one remains. They finished two of the houses in 1860 but, oddly, did not build the third house until 1903. They designated the house on the left as the "first keeper's dwelling and the one on the right as "assistant keepers' dwelling." Since the station had two assistant keepers, why did they not build three dwellings in the beginning? The Lighthouse Board certainly could have afforded it. Imagine how cramped that small cottage would have been for two families. Both of

Fig. 26: Brick oil house. Photo by John Bailey.

A Tour of the Grounds

the buildings are identical. An inspection dated 1878[24] describes them:

> "There are two keepers' dwellings; the foundation and cellar walls are of brick and buildings are frame, lathed and plastered inside, one and a half stories high; first story is divided into 3 rooms and entry with stairway, porch in front, and enclosed shed over back door; the second floors are divided into 4 rooms. There are cellars under each house, paved with brick; the buildings are well supplied with closets throughout; there is one well between the houses, and no cistern."

Every year, the Lighthouse Board inspected and reported on the station. Reports from as early as 1880 plead that the site needs another dwelling. Two families had to crowd into one house, and use the same kitchen. The reports request an addition, "which will cost $2000." Apparently these requests fell on deaf ears, as subsequent reports from 1896 through 1900 repeated this plea for additional lodging:[25]

> "This is a first-order seacoast light, and three keepers are employed to attend it. There are quarters for only two families and the third keeper has to be accommodated by makeshift arrangements which are thoroughly unsatisfactory and detrimental to the discipline and efficiency of the service. It is estimated that an additional keeper's dwelling can be built here at a cost not exceeding $4,000, and it is recommended that an appropriation of that amount be made herefor."

Finally, in 1902 work began on the third keeper's dwelling. In 1903, the second assistant and his family moved into private accommodations. For some reason, the contractors built the new structure as an addition onto the assistant keeper's dwelling (see Fig. 22) and of a completely different design. It looks like they just tacked it on to the side of the old building. This ruined the symmetry of the site.

The 1907 inspection describes the new dwelling as a frame house with brick foundation, 48' 7" from the tower, 8 rooms and a bath.[26] Compare the dwelling on the right in Figure 25 with the same dwelling as it was built in 1903. What a change! Apparently, someone renovated it at some point to make it look less "built-on." This still did nothing to improve the site's symmetry.

An unknown vandal (perhaps an irate student of rhythmic

Fig. 27: Lighthouse site with burned keepers' dwelling in ruins. Photo from the collection of H. Gerald MacDonald.

architecture) burned the newer dwelling in 1968. After the loss, the state stationed a permanent ranger at the park to protect the property.

Oil House

In order to reduce fumes and the risk of fire in the tower, the government constructed the brick oil house. Built in 1893, the oil

A Tour of the Grounds

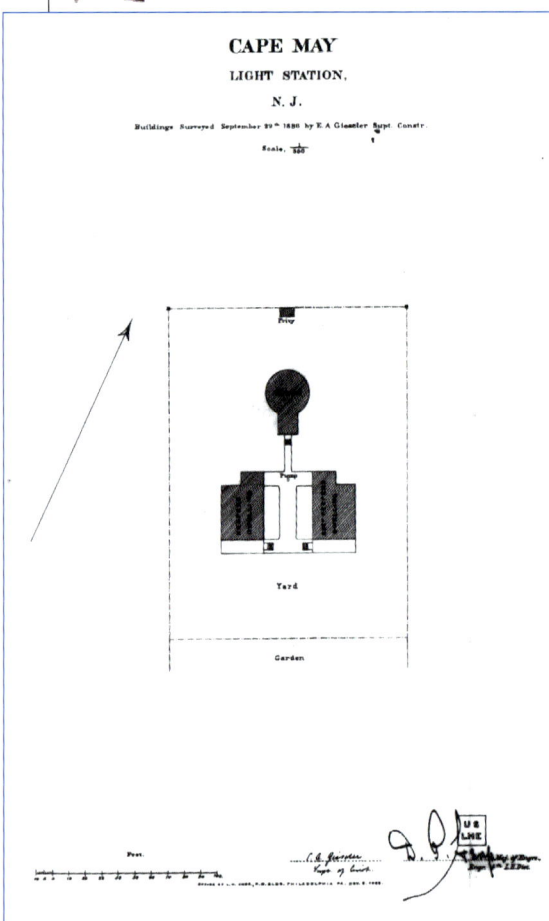

Fig. 28: 1886 Survey detail showing privy location. Illustration courtesy of MAC.

house allowed the keepers to move the bulk oil, previously stored in the vestibule, outside of the tower. They stored the oil in 5-gallon oil butts or cans. The oil house measures 14 feet by 18 feet and originally had a brick floor. The keepers removed the original brick floor so that sand could soak up the spilled oil. The last keeper, Harry Palmer, an avid gardener, complained that he could never get anything to grow around the oil house because of its contaminated soil. The building once contained a large oil tank. After electrification, the oil house had no function other than to house the emergency generator system, but even that has been removed. The Mid-Atlantic Center for the Arts (MAC) presently uses the oil house as an orientation center and museum shop.

Earlier Buildings

When they demolished the 1847 Lighthouse, the Engineers retained about 8 feet of the old tower, built a roof over it, and used it for cold storage. They even recycled the old keeper's dwelling and used it for stables. This entire area is now at the present water line. The stables and the base of the old lighthouse have broken into pieces and washed away.

Three frame privies served as the toilet facilities for the complex. They were simply small frame houses, containing a box for a seat with a lid-covered oval opening, standing over a deep pit. They were the predecessors of the common "Port-o-lets" found at present construction sites or festivals. Old documents (see Fig. 28) and pictures have located the site of the former privies and current restoration plans call for recreating them at their original location.

48

KEEPERS OF THE LIGHT

"Anythin' for a quiet life, as the man said wen he took the sitivation (sic) at the lighthouse"
- Charles Dickens

There have always been those who choose to make their way through this world with danger and loneliness for companions. Invariably they acquire the kind of mystique that surrounds cowboys, miners, seafarers, railroad engineers ... and lighthouse keepers. These souls and their yarns make up the stuff of folk songs, legends, and heroes. Here's to those among 'em who chose to be keepers of the Cape May light!

Evolution Of The Keeper

Lighthouse keepers have always had a fine reputation for devotion to their duties. For the most part, they have deserved this reputation. However, they had a rough beginning.

Political Appointees

Prior to the formation of the Lighthouse Board, politicians appointed keepers (see page 101). Congressmen and local politicians saw a lighthouse in their district as a plum. Consequently, they didn't always appoint the best qualified people. Local political favoritism could, for example, even result in a fine keeper losing his

Watching the Light

Keepers of the Light

Keeper Downes E. Foster
Photo courtesy of MAC

position to the mayor's brother-in-law. Stephen Pleasanton's administration had the local collectors of customs (themselves political appointees) investigate any charges against keepers. Hopefully, the keeper under investigation had loyalties to the local party (or was related to the mayor).

Obviously, this was not the best way to build a dedicated service. The investigation of 1851 included a close look at those who kept the lights.

Lighthouse Board Investigation

The Board's report found the interest and ability of keepers "was very various" and recommended steps to minimize the effects of politics on keepers. Cape May's report shows that we may have had the political problem here in Cape May! The keeper, Mr. Downes E. Foster, "...took charge April, 1850; removed predecessor; had no training or experience before taking charge..." (See Appendix C for the complete report.) Even with a limited knowledge of politics, Mr. Foster does look suspicious.

Besides the political appointment system, the lack of instructions and inadequate training were two things that struck the investigators as wrong.

Developing the Proper Keeper

The lighthouse board eliminated the appointee system. They instituted comprehensive testing followed by a compulsory probation period. They printed manuals and instructions covering every aspect of the keepers' duties in minute detail. They required that prospective keepers not only know how to read, but to fully comprehend everything they read.

Once out of the probation period, personnel worked their way through the ranks at each assignment from second assistant to the coveted position of fully qualified (head) keeper. Once qualified, they usually assumed the keeper position at new assignments.

In 1884, the board approved and issued snappy uniforms that rivaled those of the naval services. Keepers' dress blues included coat, vest, trousers, and cap. Two rows of shiny brass buttons accent the double breasted coat. The front of the cap features a gold and silver lighthouse badge centered above the shiny black visor. In the summer, keepers sported a light blue uniform with an optional canvas sun helmet. Note Harry Palmer's striped tie in Fig. 29.

President Grover Cleveland issued a proclamation dated May 6, 1896, that moved the nation's lighthouse keepers into the classified Civil Service System. Highly efficient, dedicated, career personnel now filled the field of lighthouse keepers. The keepers manning the Cape May Lighthouse at the turn of the 20th century were proud members of an elite corps, the finest lighthouse system in the world.

In 1918 the service changed all the ranking positions of first assistant keeper, second assistant keeper, assistant keeper, and so on, to simply keeper.

Job Description and Wages

Basically, the keeper had a simple job to keep the light brightly lighted and flashing at its specified interval. Navigators out on the dark sea identify each lighthouse by the interval of its flash. Any variation of that interval could result in a misidentification and a catastrophe. The keepers had similar responsibilities to modern air traffic controllers.

The keepers stood watches in the watch room keeping the light

Keepers of the Light

in sight and tended all night, every night. Should snow begin to cover the lantern's windows, the keepers climbed about outside, clearing the glass, like human windshield wipers.

Lighthouse keepers assisted in sea rescue operations. The service encouraged them to grow gardens, making them as self-sufficient as possible in their isolated locations. The keepers maintained their station's grounds and buildings with a seaman's meticulousness. They washed the lantern's windows inside and out. They polished all of the brass fixtures. They painted their lighthouse regularly, right up to the ball on top of the roof. The service inspected their station on a regular basis and reported the results to Washington. They received an average annual salary of $600 ($50 a month) plus room and board, a pretty good salary for their time. In 1898, the national average annual income was $440. A 3-bedroom home cost $2200; a dozen eggs, 20¢; a gallon of milk, 27¢.

Fig. 29: Young Harry Palmer in dress uniform. Photo courtesy of the Palmer family.

Cape May's Keepers

The following list includes all of the known (Head) keepers at this station and their annual salaries:[27]

Ephraim Mills	Probably 1823	(Salary unknown)
Ezekiel Stevens	Before 1847	(Salary unknown)
Downes E. Foster	April, 1850	(Salary unknown)
Wm. C. Gregory	Sept. 22, 1853	$400
Downes E. Foster	March 26, 1861	$720
Samuel Stilwell	Sept. 4, 1877	$760
Caleb S. Woolson	Oct. 1, 1903	$760
Harry H. Palmer	May 1924	$960

Ephraim Mills is the first known keeper of the 1823 Lighthouse. A journalist that visited the lighthouse in 1828 described Mills as an "old pilot."[28] We have no idea exactly when Ezekiel Stevens relieved Mr. Mills, but Ezekiel was on-site during the construction of the 1847 Lighthouse. He sketched the original map (Appendix E) during that construction period, and marked the location of the "old tower" clearly. Stevens remained on as keeper of that lighthouse until Downes E. Foster's political appointment removed him. We will probably never know whether Ezekiel asked for relief or had to be carried off the site kicking and screaming.

Keeper Downes E. Foster and wife, Ann (Hughes) Foster near the end of their second tenure. Photo courtesy of MAC.

William Gregory replaced keeper Foster at a time (1853) that looks suspiciously like an action of the Lighthouse Board. And, from their inspection report on Cape May, it seems likely. We have no details of his absence from the rolls from 1853 until his reappointment; but if the Board did remove him for his "lack of training," he apparently redeemed himself. They reappointed him as keeper here on March 26, 1861.

Two of these keepers, Samuel Stilwell and Caleb S. Woolson, worked their way up through the ranks of assistant keeper at the Cape May Light Station.

Samuel Stilwell arrived at this station September 14, 1859, as first

Keepers of the Light

Fig. 31:
Letter to the last custodian, Mrs. H.H. Palmer

assistant. He served as first assistant until promoted to keeper in 1877. By the time that he resigned in 1903, Sam had dedicated 44 years of his life to the Cape May Lighthouse. "Samuel Stilwell, for 27 years captain of the Cape May Lighthouse retires today from government service on account of advanced age. He will be 80 on Christmas. 'I can still climb the lighthouse,' he said, '200 steps, but I got rheumatism in the calf of my leg.'"[29]

Caleb S. Woolson arrived here on May 14, 1842. He served faithfully as first assistant to Samuel Stilwell until he received his promotion to keeper. A serious fall in 1902 didn't affect his dedication, "Swain Woolson, assistant keeper of the Cape May Lighthouse, fell from the top of a 15-foot ladder on Saturday last, breaking his wrist and injuring his hip." He received his promotion to keeper a year later. When Harry Palmer relieved him in 1924, Caleb had spent 37 years carrying oil up the 217 steps of this tower every night.

The last keeper of the Cape May lighthouse, Harry Hall Palmer, arrived here from Cape Henlopen October first, 1924 and retired on disability, July 1, 1933, following a serious heart attack. When Mr. Palmer assumed his duties here, he carried oil up these steps to light the lamp. When he retired, electricity lighted the lamp. He must have had an exciting and interesting tour of duty. He received retirement pay of "$1,106.95 per annum."[30]

Harry remained on the site with his wife, Florence Arabelle (Jeffreys), who served as custodian at the lighthouse through December of 1935 when she requested a replacement (see letter Figure 31)

The Palmers' ninth child, Ada, recalls life at the Cape May light station as a young girl. The Coast Guard moved the family from their previous duty station, Cape Henlopen, on a Lighthouse Tender. A gale whipped up the bay during the crossing and most of the family spent the voyage hanging their green faces over the rail. Ada immediately fell in love with Cape May, but her older sister Ida had many friends in Lewes, and hated the move. She never adapted to life in Cape May as a young girl.

Mr. Palmer loved gardening. During his tenure here, the station's lawns and gardens flourished. His hydrangeas regularly won blue ribbons at the Cape May flower show in Convention Hall. Ada's job was to keep grass out of the beautiful brick walks, a back-breaking and boring job for a vital young girl. One summer, Ada salted the cracks to slow down the aggressive

Fig. 32: Children on the beautiful brick sidewalk Kenneth, Charles, and Doris Schmierer, and the Repp twins, Ruth and Dorothy (staying with the Palmers). Photo courtesy of the Palmer family.

Fig 33. The Palmers: Florence, Florence Arabelle (Belle), Harry Hall, and Ada at the keepers residence (winter 1933). Photo courtesy of the Palmer family.

Keepers of the Light

grasses and, hopefully, to save her more time for the beach. Soon the inevitable permanent white salt stains began creeping across the bricks. Her father was not amused.

One of the keepers' more unpleasant tasks was to paint the lighthouse, including the roof and the ventilator ball on top of it. According to Ada, her father had no fear. He simply placed a ladder on the watch gallery, tossed a loop of rope around the ventilator ball, and went aloft to paint. She couldn't watch.

These wonderful people lived out their lives here at the Cape May Lighthouse. They worked hard and had great pride in their station. I've often wondered if the old lighthouse had any ghost stories attached to it. There seems to be none. From what I've heard of ghosts, an unhappy lifetime leaves its ghost behind to resolve some problem here on earth. Could it be that those who spent their lives beneath the light's sweeping glow had a contentment that few of us share today? Could it be that they were all totally happy with their lot in life? It certainly seems that way whenever one talks to their descendants. They all have fond memories of the Cape May Lighthouse.

However, the second keeper's cottage is another story. It seems to have had some sort of weird haunt! It started out as an exact duplicate of its neighbor. Then some kind of nonmatching attachment was built onto it. The next picture shows a totally different structure standing in its place. Finally, it burned to the ground, leaving nothing but its cellar foundation, and a lonely First keeper's cottage. Surely that house had some kind of karma attached to it. Can an inanimate form be unhappy?

In 1935, Harry and Belle Palmer left the station and moved into an apartment upstairs at 656 Washington Street in Cape May City. It was there that Harry died. The last keeper had gone.

Harry Palmer ready to go aloft to paint the roof of the lighthouse. Photo courtesy of the Palmer family.

AFTER THE KEEPERS LEFT

"The keepers don't come here any more."
"Sentinel of the Jersey Cape" Video

Exactly who kept the Cape May Lighthouse after the Palmers' retirement in 1935 is pretty sketchy. The descendants of the keepers say that they thought the Coast Guard took over. In 1933 the lighthouse became electrified which somewhat limited the job of keeper. Then, in 1938 the service installed an automatic electric lamp. If a bulb burns out, another moves into its place without skipping a beat, thus eliminating the need for a permanently stationed keeper.

World War II

The president didn't consolidate the Bureau of Lighthouses and the U.S. Coast Guard until July 7, 1939. That same year, on September 1, Nazi Germany invaded Poland, touching off World War II in Europe. On September 8, President Roosevelt declared a "limited national emergency" in response to the outbreak of war. Shortly after that, the Cape May Lighthouse site, already a Coast Guard base, became an armed camp.

The light was discontinued throughout the war as a part of Civil Defense measures. The entire country was blacked out, especially along the coast, every night. Any light along the shore (and for some distance inland) would silhouette American ships as they hugged the coast line. Any hapless ship silhouetted by a light ashore would allow German U-Boat (submarine) skippers to sight and torpedo it. Every home had black curtains or the occupants sat in the dark. Flash lights, street lights, car lights, and traffic lights were all turned off. Civil defense volunteers combed the neighborhoods looking for any light that might shine around a curtain in a home or office. Even lighting a cigarette outdoors at night would bring the volunteers running.

After the Keepers Left

Fig. 34: The World War II Bunker in 1999. It was originally built underground among the dunes. Photo by John Bailey

The Army built a huge gun emplacement near the lighthouse with a fortified bunker behind it back in the dunes and underground, so all that one could see through the dunes were the guns themselves. Fortunately, they were never fired in anger, only for target practice.[31]

The U.S. military built lookout towers south and north of the lighthouse, and a lookout platform inside the lighthouse just below the watch room. The location in the lighthouse allowed lookouts to spot shipping through the port holes between the granite brackets above, a heavily fortified position. The watch towers had reinforced concrete sides with a slit near the top facing the sea. From these three spotting locations, the lookouts could triangulate and find the exact position of an enemy ship trying to enter the Delaware Bay. During the war years the station bristled with activity. Afterwards, the Army abandoned Cape May.

Today, the Army's great bunker has been washed from its hiding place in the dunes and stands at sea upon its spindly pilings. It too faces the same fate as the earlier lighthouses that have stood here. A good storm and it would be gone. Perhaps that storm has already taken the bunker as you read this.

The lookout towers stand gaunt and empty with graffiti here and there. One stands on the left side of Sunset Boulevard on the way to the concrete ship. A lonely marker whom time has forgotten. The other has been surrounded by a hotel (at Beach and Philadelphia Avenue). It stares out to sea over the roof top of the hotel as if it still has a mission.

58

Post War Coast Guard

After the war ended, the Army decommissioned the base, hauled down their flag, and drove their last truck and jeep up Sunset Boulevard for points north. The Coast Guard settled into the old Lifesaving Station and assumed the maintenance duties for the Lighthouse. In 1948, after the Navy abandoned their Sewell's Point base, the Coast Guard deserted the old Lifesaving Station and moved to the Navy base, their present base, in Cape May City. After all, the lighthouse had a new automatic beacon (installed in 1946) and an emergency generator. It could practically run itself. In 1960, the encroaching ocean undermined the Lifesaving Station building itself and, as a final blow, someone torched it just before it would have toppled into the sea.

However, the Coast Guard did take good care of the old lighthouse, painting and cleaning it with military thoroughness and neatness. They stood inspections at the lighthouse regularly, and report-

Fig. 35: Lookout Towers.
Left: The tower is enveloped by a hotel on Beach Drive in Cape May.
Right: The tower near Cape May Point on Sunset Blvd.
Photos by John Bailey.

After the Keepers Left

ed their results to Washington. Things stayed pretty quiet at the Cape May Lighthouse until technology again reared its ugly head just as it had reared up over the earlier lighthouses that stood here. Navigation advances have steered this lighthouse and all of its peers into the wake of the tall ships. Modern seafarers, even small boaters with radios and pocketsized global positioning system (GPS) devices can pinpoint their location, to within inches of any spot on the earth. Detailed charts plot every rock and shoal in the sea. As a backup, the lights still have importance; however, a flashing aerobeacon perched atop a monopole can now perform the same job at a fraction of the cost as this proud lady standing defiantly at the tip of the Cape May peninsula. (And, at a fraction of the elegance.)

In 1964 the Coast Guard gave the Cape May Lighthouse/Lifesaving Station to the State of New Jersey for park land. The Coast Guard retained ownership of the Lighthouse. In 1968, an unknown arsonist burned one of the keepers dwellings. This forced the State to assign a permanent ranger to live at the park. His family moved into the remaining dwelling.

Government spending cut-backs, affecting all military services, hit the Coast Guard particularly hard. The organization already had an expensive full-time job keeping their once-proud network of aging lighthouses operational. These cut-backs presented a dilemma to the Coast Guard. They could no longer afford to maintain the bricks and mortar of their old lighthouses, yet they still had to maintain a system of navigational lights along the coast. So, they gave up on the towers and just serviced the lights. Wherever the old lights themselves fail, the Coast Guard usually bolts aerobeacons to the railings of their watch decks in place of the original light.

On June 15, 1973, the State of New Jersey placed the Cape May Lighthouse on the State Registry of Historic Sites. The following

November 12, the Department of the Interior followed suit and placed the lighthouse on the National Registry of Historic Sites. The Cape May Lighthouse became recognized as the landmark it is, a *national historic landmark*.

But, the lighthouse continued to deteriorate. Paint fell from the masonry and from the metal of the lantern. Rust, which never sleeps (especially near the ocean), displayed its handywork on the lantern, watch room and watch deck. Virtually every window leaked. The lighthouse desperately needed help. It was becoming an eyesore instead of a landmark.

From out of the blue, a solution presented itself: everyone began falling in love with lighthouses! Non-profit organizations, states, and individuals began to petition the Coast Guard to let them take over the towers and open them to the public.

The Restoration of the Lighthouse

In Cape May, Coast Guard Commander (now Captain, retired) Thomas Carroll approached the Board of Directors of the Mid-Atlantic Center for the Arts (MAC) with the idea of taking over the responsibility for the lighthouse from the Coast Guard. The board was less than enthusiastic about Tom's proposal. Lively discussions with lots of table pounding followed for weeks. The board already had more than it could handle with an aging historic building, the Emlen Physick Estate. It didn't need additional property that even the U.S. government couldn't afford. Tom persisted and, with unprecedented gentleness and patience, sold his idea to the board.

Fig. 36: Grand opening of the tower to the public, May 28, 1988. Photos courtesy of MAC.

61

After the Keepers Left

A complicated lease arrangement followed. In December of 1986, MAC subleased the lighthouse from the State of New Jersey, Department of Environmental Protection, Division of Parks and Forestry, who in turn had leased it from the Coast Guard. The Coast Guard retains responsibility for the light itself.

MAC opened the base of the tower to visitors that summer (1986) with a museum shop in the vestibule oil rooms. Over 46,000 people visited the tower that summer when they could only see the ground floor. They bought "Save the Lighthouse" T-shirts, certificates for bricks, landings, windows and other memorabilia. Some donated cash outright to help with the expensive restoration to come. Thousands of lighthouse lovers purchased the bricks at $2.00 apiece to help support the effort. Local organizations purchased the more expensive pieces of the lighthouse: New Jersey Bell Telephone Company bought the first window for $500 and the Coast Guard Officers' Wives Club bought the first $100 step. My mother dedicated a $500 window to her late husband "Skip DeBeneditto Torpedoman 2nd class, submarine service, US Navy," and I wrote the first edition of this book and donated its proceeds to the Lighthouse restoration effort. Like a teenager with her first real "paying job," the lighthouse began to show that she could support herself.

The Lighthouse Committee joined forces with Watson and Henry Associates,[32] restoration architects, to formulate a bold, comprehensive 10-year, $300,000 plan for carefully restoring the tower to her former glory. They focused on restoring it to the description in an inspection report dated July 26 and November 19, 1907.[33]

As the first step toward that end, MAC applied for state approval to allow the public to climb the tower. With full access to the tower, MAC could begin to charge an admission fee that, in

Personalities at the ribbon cutting (left to right):are NJ Senator, James Hurley; NJ Secretary of State, Jane Burgio; NJ Dir. Of Parks and Forestry, Greg Marshall; U.S. Congressman William Hughes; NJ Tourism Promotional Representative, Eileen Thornton; Lighthouse Committee Chairman, Thomas Carroll; President of MAC, Larry Eppler; and Commanding Officer, U.S. Coast Guard Training Center Cape May, Captain Edward Cain.

addition to museum sales, would make raising the restoration funds much easier. The state required an additional handrail and lighting for the spiral stairway, a secure cage around the watch room gallery, and miscellaneous public protection details. The organization installed the required safety features, removed piles of accumulated debris and non-historic materials, and installed informative museum signs. They had to do all of this without damaging the surfaces of the tower in any way. For example, a sign describing the view from a certain window could not be screwed into the wall next to that window. The sign had to hang from a weighted cable dropped into the vent hole at that window. These MAC volunteers scrubbed, cleaned, trained their guides, and made the Cape May Lighthouse ready for her first visitors.

On Saturday, May 28, 1988, at 11 o'clock in the morning, a ribbon cutting ceremony officially opened the tower to an adoring audience. The descendants of the keepers sat proudly in the front row. Federal, state and local dignitaries spoke in support of the

After the Keepers Left

restoration effort. The Coast Guard Band played Sousa marches under a blazing sun while Coast Guard helicopters performed their famous "fly by." Dogs barked. A "Victorian" lady cut and served a Cape May Lighthouse cake. And, despite a record Memorial Day heat wave, the door to the tower swung open and hundreds of visitors lined up to climb to the top. They were the first civilians in almost fifty years to trace the steps of the keepers up her curved staircase to the watch room. Thousands followed those first climbers and she really began to pay her way. The dream of saving the Cape May Lighthouse began to look like a reality.

The reality hit a stone wall immediately when ownership of the lighthouse loomed as a problem. It seems that since the Coast Guard (the Federal Government) owned the lighthouse, it was not eligible for any state grant money. The New Jersey Historic Trust, for example, had money earmarked for restoration projects in South Jersey but couldn't give it to a property owned by the Federal Government. The Lighthouse Committee called on Representative William J. Hughes, who sponsored federal legislation to transfer ownership of the lighthouse to the New Jersey Department of Environmental Protection (DEP).

In a ceremony at the base of the lighthouse, on a beautiful Saturday, September 19, 1992, the ownership of the lighthouse passed from the Coast Guard to the State of New Jersey. For the first time ever, the red, white and blue U.S. Coast Guard flag slowly descended from the top of the lighthouse while the gold and blue flag of New Jersey ascended to fly from the top of the tower. Immediately following the ceremonial title transfer, James F. Hall, Assistant Commissioner for Natural and Historic Resources presented a check for $19,962 to MAC president John Bailey. "MAC will now be able to see the grants that they've worked so hard to get," Hall said. "It did take a lot of effort and a lot of dedication!"

An orange Coast Guard helicopter performed a thundering fly-by while the Training Center band performed "America the Beautiful" and a large American flag unfurled from the watch gallery. Many wiped tears of patriotic joy from their eyes.

In February, 1993, MAC received a matching grant of $197,842 from the New Jersey Historic Trust. Then in March, MAC received an outright grant of $316,000 for restoration of the Cape May Lighthouse from the Department of Transportation ISTEA ("iced tea") fund, the Federal Intermodal Surface Transportation Efficiency Act. The act earmarks money for improving transportation related projects such as bike ways, hiking paths, road landscaping and historic preservation of transportation related structures. With $526,000 in two grants, the Lighthouse Committee began in earnest to look for a restoration contractor and put the project out to bid. The committee selected the International Chimney Corporation[34] of Buffalo, New York, to do the work.

Since the restoration of the lantern required that the lighthouse be darkened for the first time since World War II, the Coast Guard had to announce that fact in their *Notice to Mariners* publication. And, should any sailors have a problem with the Cape being in darkness for the entire winter, the Coast Guard was willing to consider the sailor's problem at a public hearing. The hearing could have resulted in the denial of permission to turn out the light. Oddly, they received not one comment. It may have been unusual, but it was a blessing for the project!

In the meantime, Watson and Henry scraped the tower's paint down to its original layers to find out if the tower had always been white. As it turned out, it hadn't. The original color was a cement wash, sort of a cream color. That too had to be approved by the Coast Guard as mariners identify a lighthouse in the daytime (its "day mark") by its color. The Coast Guard didn't see that much dif-

After the Keepers Left

Fig. 37: The "can" atop the tower. Photo by John Bailey.

ference in the new color and signed off right away. However, the Cape May rumor mill went on a streak. MAC's phones rang daily with complaints. Citizens interrupted City Council meetings in Cape May and Cape May Point demanding that MAC not change the color of their beloved lighthouse to the rumored blue. MAC representatives gently reassured everyone that they had no intention of painting the lighthouse blue. Blue, the color of the sky, would make the lighthouse virtually invisible as a day mark. (Who would start this kind of rumor? Who would believe it?) The uproar gradually died down and the restoration began.

In December, 1993, International Chimney rolled onto the site with a magnificent crane. It dwarfed the lighthouse! The architect's plans called for removing the lantern intact and shipping it

66

to International's warehouse in Buffalo where experts could restore it at leisure and in comfort.

In preparation, workers removed all of the bolts holding the lantern to the tower. The crane braced to lift the lantern, but nothing happened. The builders had built the vertical window dividers deep into the masonry of the tower. The lantern was part of the tower. It was going nowhere. The architects decided to completely dismantle the lantern, including the roof and windows, and send all of the parts, except for the vertical window dividers off to Buffalo. The crane gingerly lifted the 3400 pound roof from the lantern and slowly lowered it onto a flat bed trailer for its trip to Buffalo. After releasing the roof, the crane again swung back to the top of the tower, lifted the revolving light apparatus and lowered it to a waiting Coast Guard truck. The Guard took the light to their workshops for a complete overhaul. Finally, the contractor placed a gigantic 7,000 pound, 16-foot by 12-foot, dark green, metal "can" over the top of the tower. Their crews could now work inside the can on the watch room and all that was left of the lantern in relative comfort throughout the winter of 1994, the coldest winter in the collective memory of the cape.

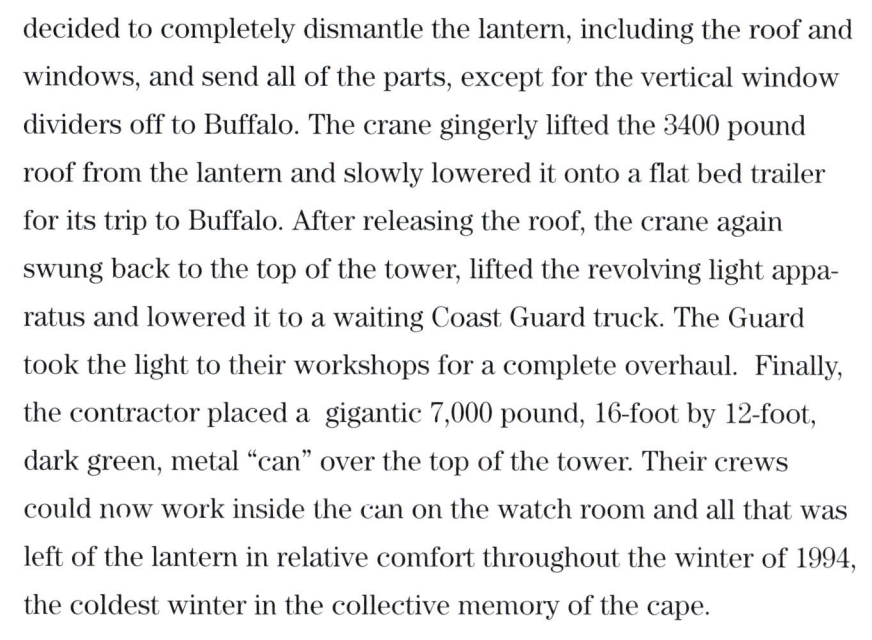

All winter long workers removed the rust from the watch room and gallery, and repainted the old lens base. They stripped the peeling paint from the tower and repainted it with a cement-like coating, brand named MODAC. From the outside, the tower began to look like it must have looked to the Army Engineer inspectors in 1907.

Finally, the day for the return of the roof arrived. It was a beau-

Fig. 38: Coast Guardsmen rig the light for its return to the top. Photo by John Bailey.

After the Keepers Left

Fig. 39: The roof with its rough weld joints stands before the can on the ground. Photo by John Bailey.

tiful spring day, perfect for lifting the roof back into its rightful place at the top of the lantern. The crane first lifted the can from the tower and lowered it to the ground. The Coast Guard, who had arrived early, rigged a sling on the newly refurbished light and the crane picked it up from the back of their truck and smoothly replaced it in the lantern where the guardsmen reinstalled it in its old location.

The truck carrying the roof was late, caught in traffic. Workers and onlookers shuffled nervously. Suddenly, the welcome roar of a big diesel truck engine shifting its gears on Lighthouse Avenue echoed through the crisp morning air. The lead car turned into the park followed by the flatbed tractor-trailer. The roof looked beautiful. It sparkled, bright red in the sunlight. Riggers swarmed over the trailer, removing its tiedowns and making preparations to lift the roof from the truck. The architect climbed up on the truck and began running his fingers over the weld joints and talking with the riggers. He jumped down and began an animated conversation with the contractors. They were all talking at once, shaking their heads, pointing at the truck, and kicking dirt around. What was going on? Had the roof failed Michael Henry's inspection? If so, would it have to go back to Buffalo?

The roof had failed inspection. The joints were too rough to hold paint. However, Michael decided to bring in a local craftsman to repair it here, on site. That craftsman was Steve Bradway,

68

a fine metalsmith who excels at everything from copper gutters to tin roofs and even copper pots and pans. Steve spent two days soldering, polishing and grinding the weld joints until they were as smooth as the rest of the roof. The contractor's painters finished the job and the roof was ready!

The next morning dawned clear and bright with a light breeze. Perfect for replacing the roof on the lantern. All eyes and cameras were trained on the crane. The crane's engine revved and strained as the red crown of the lighthouse began to rise above the trees to the delighted applause of the crowd. Refitting it to the lantern proved to be a bit of a chore; getting everything lined up just right seemed almost impossible. The crane held the roof just above the lantern as precisely as if giant human fingers were gently nudging it about. Finally, the first bolts began to drop into place and the workers began to signal thumbs up. The lighthouse was slowly coming back together. It was beginning to look like our Cape May Lighthouse again. They replaced the windows with safety glass, thus eliminating the need for bird netting around the lantern.

With the lantern all buttoned up with all of its windows replaced and the ventilator ball atop the roof back in place and tightened down all the way around, the lighthouse was again ready for visitors. But, not without one of MAC's famous ceremonies.

On June 11, 1994, at 3:00 in the afternoon, the Lighthouse Committee held a Grand Reopening Ceremony with illustrious speakers and the ubiquitous United States Coast Guard Training Center Band. Everyone attending received a free ticket to climb

Fig. 40: Touching up the roof's weld joints. Photo by John Bailey.

After the Keepers Left

Fig. 41: Nudging the roof back into place. Photo by John Bailey.

the newly refurbished lighthouse and enjoyed light refreshments.

The museum shop reopened in the restored oil house where the Coast Guard had removed the emergency generator system, deeming it no longer necessary. This delighted the shopkeepers who now had much more room with no generator to work around and keep hidden from view.

Strangely, exactly one year later, June 11, 1995, at 1:30 in the afternoon, a visitor to the lighthouse from Lancaster, Pennsylvania, squeezed through the bars of the observation deck and leaped to his death from the tower. Police called the fall an apparent suicide. Lower Township Detective Ed Donohue said that the narrow bars securing the observation area at the top of the lighthouse virtually ruled out the possibility that his death was accidental. The questions of how he climbed outside of the tight iron grill surrounding the gallery and if he knew that he had chosen the exact anniversary of the reopening of the lighthouse remain unanswered.

Another mystery began playing its mischief in the lantern. With every rain shower, water filled the drip pans inside the windows and puddled randomly in the watch room below. I personally climbed the lighthouse with every shower or heavy nor'easter and tried to catch the pesky water sneaking into the lantern to no avail. The architect, suspecting that the caulk had failed, had the contractor remove the windows and recaulk them, with no success. The water continued to fill drip pans and puddle on the floor. The ventilator ball had to be the culprit. Pressure water tests on all sides of the ball failed to produce even one drop inside. However, the water tests showed that the roof itself had baffling leaks. They would have to be repaired in place.

MAC applied successfully for another round of grants. The New Jersey Department of Transportation awarded the lighthouse a new ISTEA grant of $404,097; and, the New Jersey Historic Trust, administered by the Department of Environmental Protection awarded the lighthouse a $512,594 grant. MAC was now ready for the next phase of the restoration.

In the winter of 1998, after the bulk of seasonal visitors had left the lighthouse empty and alone again, Masonry Preservation Group[35] (MPG) of Merchantville, New Jersey, parked their crane next to the lighthouse. They used a different technique than International Chimney. They had a smaller crane, and used it to build scaffolding around the lantern. The men worked from the scaffolding. The crane simply hoisted them and their materials to and from the top of the tower.

Fig. 42: Scaffolding surrounds the Lantern. Photo by Nancy Bailey.

MPG performed the water tests on the lantern and repaired the leaks. They adjusted the security grill that covers the outer watch deck to increase the level of protection to the public. They completely restored the watch room, stripping away coats of old paint, replacing the floor, and varnishing the woodwork. When they lifted the floor to replace it, they discovered the beautiful original radial flooring beneath it (see Fig 12). MPG cleaned and repointed the stone foundation. Then they painted the spiral stairway.

After the Keepers Left

When the lighthouse reopened for the 1998 season, its visitors found a restored Cape May Lighthouse that looked like it must have looked in the early 1900s... maybe even better.

Ongoing plans for the future

The ongoing plans by the Mid-Atlantic Center for the Arts call for restoring the brick sidewalks and grounds around the lighthouse, and placing educational kiosks at strategic points along the sidewalks. They hope to replace the privies in their original location. MAC is reaching out to other lighthouses along the Jersey shore, such as the Hereford Inlet Lighthouse, to set up combination tours. Visitors can now (2000) purchase one ticket and visit both lighthouses.

The "stuff of dreams" includes acquiring the remaining keeper's cottage for use as a lighthouse museum and having the great Fresnel lens returned to its rightful place, on site, in the lighthouse museum.

EPILOGUE

"The best preparation for the future is the present well seen to, and the last duty done."
- H. Gerald MacDonald

Fig. 43: The Cove. Photo by John Bailey.

As we've already discussed, beach erosion at the Cape May Point State Park is inching its way inexorably toward the base of the lighthouse. Drive down Beach Drive in Cape May City to where it abruptly ends at the cove. Admire the magnificent sweep of the cove with the Lighthouse and St. Mary's-by-the-Sea at the final point of land. The panorama is inspiring, but also frightening. The view wasn't always like this.

Beach Drive once continued straight from where you stand all the way through Cape May Point. A survey of the lighthouse site dated 1889 (see Fig. 21) includes a road seaward of both the Lifesaving Station and the trolley line with the identification,

Epilogue

"Beach Drive to Cape May City and Cape May Point." The Cape May Delaware Bay & Sewell's Point Railroad trolley line ran through here from Sewell's Point, straight across the cove, past the lighthouse all the way to the steamboat landing (the present end of Sunset Boulevard and location of the concrete ship). You are looking at the location of the lost community of South Cape May, incorporated as a borough in 1894.

South Cape May had its own mayor, many blocks of beautiful Victorian homes facing a boardwalk and a broad expanse of beach. Samuel Bailie had a house that stood between 13th and 14th Avenues. (The old Cape May boundary was at 9th Avenue and today Cape May exists only to 2nd Avenue.) By 1917, the Bailie House stood alone in South Cape May with vast meadows around it. A major storm during the winter of 1917/1918 marked the finish of the community. Today the site is about a quarter of a mile at sea. Samuel was the last to leave. He gave up and moved his home, in the spring of 1918, to 12 South Broadway in Cape May where it stands today.[36]

The cove comes and goes. In 1985, the fury of Hurricane Gloria crushed the dunes and took a huge bite out of the cove in one afternoon alone! Then, when Cape May began rebuilding its beaches, the cove snubbed its nose at the millions being spent in Cape May and filled itself in. You could walk where porpoises once played. The city posted life guards on the new beach and collected beach fees. The restaurant facing the cove complained that the dunes ruined their view and filled their parking lot with sand. The owners asked the City of Cape May to remove the dunes and the sand from their parking lot. The following year, the beach disappeared.

The Cape May Point State Park has experienced persistent deterioration of its beaches. The World War II bunker still has the

Fig. 44: Aerial view looking north from Cape May Point, ca: 1920. Notice the homes on the beach and in the surf between the lighthouse station and Cape May City. Photo from the collection of H. Gerald MacDonald.

brackets for coin operated binoculars, where visitors recently enjoyed the view, had picnics, and sat on park benches. Today, no one can even get out to the bunker. Remember that the Army built it safely *underground*, back in the dunes. Fig. 45 shows the park's last line of defense, a seawall of plastic bags fronting tidal wet sand. This was recently a dry beach. The concrete monuments are the underground cement foundations for one of the World War II radio transmission towers. In Fig. 24, the tower is the one (of the three large striped radio antennas) that is closest to the righthand edge of the photograph behind the barn and the base of the 1847 lighthouse.

Erosion is not a new problem on the Cape May peninsula. In 1805, Commodore Stephen Decatur (father of the famous naval

Epilogue

Fig. 45: The remains of the state park's beach. Photo by John Bailey.

hero), measured the distance from the highwater mark to the Atlantic Hotel (at the foot of Jackson Street in Cape May) and observed an average annual loss of nearly four feet of land. Will the persistent ocean claim this lighthouse as it has her earlier sisters? Only the future knows.

MAC's restoration plan and cash flow projection go well into the first century of the new millennium. Perhaps MAC could move the lighthouse if the need arises. Yet, I can't help but wonder if the lighthouse will survive to celebrate her 200th birth date (October 31, 2059). The future may know. But, the future of this lighthouse, at this point in time, is entirely in our hands.

As the old keepers, Downes, Caleb, and Harry would say, "You have the watch!"

Photo: Cape Publishing, Inc.

APPENDIX A

Cape May Lighthouse at a Glance

"History is philosophy teaching by example, and also by warning; its two eyes are geography and chronology."

- James Garfield, 20th President of the United States

Chronological History

1640   New England and Long Island whalers establish Portsmouth (now Town Bank, NJ), an English whaling community.

1710   The estate of Johnathan Pyne, the original colonial landowner, transfers the deed for the land (a portion of which will become the borough of Cape May Point and the State Park) to John Stites, after which it becomes known as "Stites Beach."

1744   The first lighthouse built at Cape May according to a 1954 *Cape May Star & Wave* newspaper article (see 1954).

1767   Pennsylvania Board of Port Wardens (Colonial businessmen) build a lighthouse at the south entrance to the Delaware Bay, on Cape Henlopen. Oddly as far as we know, they never built a tower on the busy north entrance to the bay, on Cape May.

1775-1781 American Revolution (American War of Independence from Great Britain).

1785   *September 23*, deed on record in Cape May Court House states, "Thomas Hand, 2nd, gentleman, conveys to the Board of Port Wardens, City of Philadelphia, ... a tract of land for the purpose of erecting thereon a beacon for the benefit of navigation." The location of the land is in front of the present Congress Hall Hotel (on Beach Drive in Cape May City).

1789   *August 7*, First Congress enacts the nation's ninth law establishing the U.S. Lighthouse Service under the Treasury Department. President George Washington signs it into law. The Lighthouse Service will be consolidated with the Coast Guard in 1939.

1790   *August 4*, First Congress establishes the Revenue Cutter Service. It will become the Coast Guard when consolidated with the Lifesaving Service in 1915.

1801   *July*, the *Philadelphia Aurora* carries the following advertisement titled, *Seashore Entertainment at Cape May*, "... The situation is beautiful, just on the confluence of Delaware Bay with the ocean, in sight of the Lighthouse, and affords a view of the shipping which enters and leaves the Delaware. ..." Yet, we know of no lighthouse being built on Cape May for 20 more years.

1802   *March 16*, Congress authorizes President Thomas Jefferson to organize the Army Corps of Engineers to be stationed at West Point. Among other duties, the corps oversees all engineering and site selection for the nation's lighthouses.

1805   Stephen Decatur Sr. (the father of the famous naval hero) measures the distance from the high-water mark to the Atlantic Hotel in Cape Island (Cape May City) and observes an annual average loss of nearly four feet of land.

1822 *July 15*, "Site conveyed for this Lighthouse was from John Stites and wife, to the United States, the consideration being $300 and the amount of land 1 acre." (From the 4th District Engineers description of the lighthouse, dated March 20, 1878.)

1823 Government builds first known Cape May Lighthouse. It stands 68 feet tall. The encroaching ocean forces the government to move the Lighthouse further inland in 1847. Its original location is in the ocean about 100 yards off shore from the present St. Mary's by the Sea. Ephraim Mills is the first known keeper of this Lighthouse. He was there in 1828 when a journalist for the *West Jersey Observer* visited the site and described him as an old pilot. Ezekiel Stevens relieved Ephraim at some point before 1847.

1836 Alexander Whilldin marries Jane G. Stites and receives the land previously owned by the Stites family as dowry. The land includes what is now the present community of Cape May Point, the Cape May Point State Park, and bird sanctuary.

1847 *April 9*, deed transfers land for second Lighthouse, from "Alexander Whilldin and wife, to the United States" for $1,150. The Middletons, local contractors, rebuild the first lighthouse further from the encroaching ocean on the Whilldin land, and add 10' to its height bringing it to a stately 78'. At the direction of the Lighthouse Board, the corps replaces this second Cape May Lighthouse in 1859 because it is "inadequate for the needs of commerce." The location of the second lighthouse is now just beyond the present waterline.

1848 Congress appropriates $10,000 for the purpose of placing lifesaving equipment along the New Jersey coast. They place the equipment on lighthouse stations, so that keepers as well as volunteers can work together to maintain it and save lives.

1849 Lifesaving boat house installed at Cape May Lighthouse site. The keeper is Lewis Stevens.

1850 *April*, Downes E. Foster appointed keeper of the Lighthouse. He serves until *September 22, 1853.*

1851 Congress appoints an investigating board to examine the U.S. Lighthouse establishment which, under the Fifth Auditor of the Treasury Department, Stephen Pleasanton, had fallen into disrepair.

June 25, investigating board inspects the second Cape May Lighthouse and recommends replacement of the tower and lighting apparatus.

1853 *September 22*, William C. Gregory appointed keeper of the lighthouse. He serves through March 26, 1861.

1855 Sperm whale oil, the exclusive fuel of lighthouses becomes scarce. Its price rises from $.42 to $2.25 per gallon. The Lighthouse Service experiments with dolphin, lard and colzan oils as replacements.

1857 Army Corps of Engineers begins construction of third Lighthouse. It will cost $40,000 including the new First Order Lens which will cost approximately $15,000. The corps probably used George Gordon Meade's architectural drawings for the project, as this lighthouse is identical to several others that we know are of his design.

Cape Island incorporates as a borough.

Appendix A - Cape May Lighthouse At A Glance

1858 *April 8*, deed transfers two additional adjoining acres of land from "Alexander Whilldin and wife Jane G. to the United States" for $500.

1859 *October 31*, keeper, William C. Gregory, lights the lamp at the top of the new lighthouse for the first time. The lighthouse stands 145 feet tall and is equipped with a first order rotating beehive Fresnel Lens. Except for being dark during World War II, the light serves continuously since this date, making it the oldest continually operating lighthouse in the country. Additionally, the Cape May Lighthouse Station has never been decommissioned since 1823.

1860 Two keepers' dwellings finished.

1861 *March 26*, D.E. Foster appointed keeper of the Cape May Lighthouse. It is assumed that he is the same Downes E. Foster appointed in 1850. He serves through Sept. 4, 1877.

1861-1865 American Civil War. The war between the states. Rebels destroy or disable all Federal lighthouses in the south.

1862 Corp demolishes second lighthouse tower. They leave about 8-feet of the base for use as a storage barn.

1863 *July 3*, General George G. Meade's Army of the Potomac defeats General Robert E. Lee's Confederate forces at Gettysburg. Historians mark the battle as the turning point in the war. An interesting note: both generals were engineers before the war.

1875 *February 18*, State of New Jersey charters the Sea Grove Association. With the financial assistance of John Wanamaker, the association lays out a Presbyterian retreat that will fail and eventually become the borough of Cape May Point (see 1878).
March 15, Jane and Alexander Whilldin convey the land that is now Cape May Point to the Sea Grove Association.[37]

1876 *May-November*, U.S. Centennial Exposition in Philadelphia. The Revenue Cutter Service has a display featuring a state-of-the-art Lifesaving Station. They move the station, its house and appliances to Cape May following the closing of the Exposition.

1877 *September 4*, Samuel Stillwell is appointed keeper of the lighthouse. He serves through October 1, 1903.

1878 Kerosene becomes the fuel of choice for lighthouses; Cape May Lighthouse converts to kerosene.
Congress creates U.S. Lifesaving Service as separate from the Revenue Cutter Service and places it under the Treasury Department.
Sea Grove fails. Its citizens incorporate as Cape May Point with the opening of a new post office (see 1896).

1884 West Cape May incorporates as a borough out of Lower Township.

1893 Brick oil storage building constructed to house the volatile kerosene outside of the tower.

1894 South Cape May incorporates as a borough out of West Cape May.

1896 Cape May Point loses its incorporation. Lower Township assumes jurisdiction of the area.

1902 Incandescent oil vapor lamp installed. It replaces a Funck multiple wick first order hydraulic float lamp dated 1878.

1903 Third keeper's dwelling finished. It provides accommodations for third family.
October 1, Caleb Woolson appointed keeper of the lighthouse. He serves through May 1924.

1909 Cape May Point reincorporates as a borough (see 1896).

1910 June 17, Congress establishes Bureau of Lighthouses under the Department of Commerce.

1914-1918, World War I. (Begins with the assassination of Arch Duke Ferdinand, June 28, 1914, and ends with signing of the Armistice, Nov. 11, 1918.)

1915 *January 28*, Congress establishes U.S. Coast Guard by consolidating the Revenue Cutter Service and the Lifesaving Service.

1916 *October 14*, The Cape May Delaware Bay & Sewell's Point Railroad makes its final run.

1917 *April 11*, under executive order, Cape May Light Station with equipment and personnel transferred to the Navy Department and assigned to the Fourth Naval District.[38]
U.S. Navy builds Camp Wissahickon at the location where the Garden State Parkway now ends. 700 workers construct the camp in 25 days on lands leased (for $1.00/year) from Henry Ford and the Cape May Real Estate Company. The lease is for the duration of the war plus 6 months. The camp consists of 40 buildings, including 20 dormitories, a hospital and a 50,000 gallon water tower.

1919 *July 1*, under executive order, Cape May Light Station with its equipment and personnel returns to the jurisdiction of the Department of Commerce. (Same ref. as Apr. 11, 1917.)

1924 *May*, Harry H. Palmer appointed keeper of the Cape May Lighthouse. He serves through July 1, 1933 when he suffers a heart attack.

1926 *June 8*, the concrete ship Atlantus arrives at Cape May Point after being towed by tugboat from Pig Point, Va. It was to become part of a ferry boat dock, but strikes a shoal upon arrival and remains grounded in its present location at the end of Sunset Blvd.

1933 Bureau of Lighthouses removes the oil vapor lamp and electrifies the lighthouse.
July 1, Harry Palmer's wife, Florence Arabelle Palmer appointed Custodian of the Cape May Lighthouse after her husband's heart attack. She serves through 1935.

1938 U.S. Lighthouse service installs an automatic electric lamp. This eliminates the need for permanently stationed keepers.

1939 *July 7*, President Franklin D. Roosevelt consolidates the U.S. Coast Guard and the Bureau of Lighthouses. This returns lighthouses to the jurisdiction of the Treasury Department. Keepers may either join the Coast Guard at the same pay or remain civilian (about half choose each way).

1941-1945 World War II (September 1, 1939, Nazi Germany invades Poland; December 7, 1941, Japan attacks Pearl Harbor U.S. enters war; May 9, 1945, Germany surrenders; September 2, 1945, Japan surrenders). Cape May Lighthouse dark for the first and only time throughout the war because of the threat of German U-Boats prowling off shore. Government builds large military installation at the lighthouse site, including a gun emplacement that is now threatened by the sea. A lookout platform is built inside the lighthouse near the top.

Appendix A - Cape May Lighthouse At A Glance

1942   The Northwest Magnesite Company establishes a Cape May plant on Sunset Blvd. Dolomite and seawater when burned produce magnesite. Magnesite produces refractory brick, used for heavy industrial open hearths and electric furnaces. Only the water tower from the plant remains at this time (2000).

1945   South Cape May loses its incorporation as a borough since most of its land and cottages had washed away.

1946   U.S. Coast Guard installs present rotating beacon. They remove the historical Fresnel lens and give it to the Cape May County Historical Museum. The new beacon changes the flash from its original 30 seconds to its present frequency of 15 seconds.

1948   U.S. Coast Guard moves from Lifesaving Station to their present base, an abandoned U.S. Naval Station, at Sewell's Point.

1954   *July 8*, *Cape May Star and Wave* column states, "The first lighthouse at Cape May Point was built about 1744 on the plantation of Thomas Hand. On an old map the location is marked by the word, 'Flashlight.' Hand acquired this land from William Jeacocks on April 22, 1695, who had bought it of James Budd, one of the agents of Dr. Daniel Coxe. This light was built by the English government at the same time that it built one at Cape Henlopen... The site of this old landmark has long been washed away."

1960   U.S. Coast Guard Lifesaving Station's main building stands undermined by the sea and burns by an unknown arsonist.

1962   *March*, storm that devastates the Jersey coast demolishes the Lifesaving Station's boat house.

1964   U.S. Government gives Cape May Lighthouse property to the State of New Jersey for park land. The Coast Guard retains ownership of the lighthouse.

1968   Unknown arsonist burns the original (see 1860) and the 1903 keeper's dwellings, a duplex built on the same foundation.

1970   Local citizen activists organize and form the Mid-Atlantic Center for the Arts (MAC) to save the Emlen Physick Estate in Cape May. Their fledgling organization will eventually also save the Cape May Lighthouse.

1973   *June 15*, State of New Jersey places the lighthouse on the State Registry of Historic Sites. *November 12*, Department of the Interior places the lighthouse on the National Registry of Historic Sites.

1986   *December*, Mid Atlantic Center for the Arts (MAC) subleases the Lighthouse from the State of New Jersey, Department of Environmental Protection, Division of Parks and Forestry, who in turn had leased it from the Coast Guard. Coast Guard retains responsibility for the light itself. Watson and Henry Associates of Bridgeton, NJ, restoration architects, begin restoration plans. MAC renames the lighthouse the Cape May Point Lighthouse hoping that this will make it easier for visitors to find the site, since it is adjacent to the Borough of Cape May Point and Cape May Point State Park, both already well marked by signs and maps.

1988 *May 28, 11 am*, MAC holds a grand opening ceremony of the lighthouse tower for visitors. Many local, state, and federal dignitaries attend as well as the descendants of the keepers. The Coast Guard Band entertains the visitors, who are the first of many to climb the newly opened tower.

The descendants of the keepers, the Coast Guard, history and lighthouse buffs, as well as governmental and historical granting agencies, pressure MAC about the historical inaccuracy of changing the name to Cape May Point Lighthouse. MAC researches the historical name, finds that the government officially places names on lighthouses according to the land masses that they mark, in this case the peninsula of Cape May. MAC drops the name change.

1992 *Sept. 19*, in an official ceremony at the base of the lighthouse, the ownership of the lighthouse passes from the Coast Guard to the State of New Jersey, Department of Environmental Protection. The state could now grant restoration funds for the lighthouse.

1993 *Feb.* MAC receives a matching grant of $197,842 from the New Jersey Historic Trust.

March, MAC receives $316,000 for restoration of the Cape May Lighthouse from the Department of Transportation ISTEA (iced tea) fund, the Federal Intermodal Surface Transportation Efficiency Act. The act earmarks money for improving transportation related projects such as bike ways, hiking paths, road landscaping and historic preservation. The total restoration of the outside of the tower and lantern becomes a reality.

Summer, The Keeper's Log (official publication of the United States Lighthouse Society) Vol. IX No. 4 publishes a cover article about the Cape May Light Station by John Bailey.

1994 *Winter*, The International Chimney Corporation of Buffalo, New York, contracts the restoration project through a bid selection process. They remove the lantern roof intact and truck it to their warehouse facilities in Buffalo. They place a 7000 lb. "can" over the topless lantern room and work in relative comfort to restore the lantern during the coldest winter in Cape May's collective history. They strip the paint from the tower and repaint it with a cement-like coating, brand named MODAC.

June 11, 3:00 pm, MAC holds a "Grand Re-Opening Ceremony" at the lighthouse.

1995 *June 11*, at approximately 1:30 pm, Henry Givler from Lancaster, Pa. jumps to his death from the observation gallery. He apparently squeezed through the iron grilles at the top of the cage surrounding the gallery.

1997 With a new ISTEA grant of $404,097 administered by the New Jersey Department of Transportation and a $512,594 grant from the New Jersey Historic Trust, Department of Environmental Protection, MAC moves again to further the restoration of the lighthouse.

1998 *Winter*, the Masonry Preservation Group of Merchantville, NJ, erects scaffolding around the lantern and repairs the leaking roof. They repoint the foundation masonry. They replace the roof of the vestibule with a historically accurate tin roof. They perform major restoration to the interior of the vestibule, the stairway, and watch room.

Appendix A - Cape May Lighthouse At A Glance

Geography

Location: North side of entrance to the Delaware Bay, Cape May, New Jersey, USA. 30° 55' 50" North latitude and 74° 57'36" West longitude. Surface soil: sandy loam.

Tower: 145 ft. tall painted off-white. Conical brick masonry, 27 feet outside diameter at bottom, 13 feet 6 inch outside diameter at top.

Lantern: 12' ft tall (making the lighthouse 157½ ft. Overall with a focal plane 165 feet above mean high tide) 12 ft diameter, painted red. The rails, floor, and posts are iron. The sash bars, sills, lintels, and glass stops are bronze. The roof is sheet copper with iron joists topped by a copper ventilator ball. It was originally equipped with a 1st order, rotating **Fresnel "beehive" lens** with a 30 second flash. The lens stands 7'10" tall, has a six foot diameter, 16 flash panels, and rotated once every 8 minutes.

Lamp: Electric beacon with its own lens and a 1000 watt bulb, rotating once every 30 seconds, flashing white every 15 seconds.

Range: On a clear night (meteorological visibility of 10 nautical miles) you could conceivably site the Cape May Light from 24 nautical miles away. This is its *nominal range*. Official documentation as shown in this appendix use this distance. However, the curvature of the earth *(geographical range)* limits nominal range. If the horizon hides the light from you, you won't see it no matter how strong the light. Assuming a clear night, we can use the mariner's formula to calculate the distance at which the Cape May Light will appear on the horizon, the geographical range (GR).

$$GR = (\sqrt{\text{Height of light} \times 1.5}) + (\sqrt{\text{Height of observer's eyes} \times 1.5})$$

The light in the Cape May Lighthouse stands 165 feet above the sea. So, from the level of the sea, a ship-wrecked sailor clinging to a life preserver can see this welcome sight from 14.77 miles. However, from the deck of a sailboat 12 feet above the sea, the skipper first sees the light at 18.75 miles. And from the 75-foot high bridge of an ocean going freighter, the first mate sights the light at its full nominal range, 24 miles, limited only by visibility. For further information, see *American Practical Navigator*, U.S. Navy Hydrographic Office, H.O. Pub. No. 9, U.S. Government Printing Office, Washington: 1958, pgs 259-263.

Other buildings: Brick oil storage building (built 1893). Wooden frame keeper's house with brick foundation (built 1860).

Official Descriptions

186
SEACOAST AND DELAWARE BAY

No.	Name Character and period of light	Location Latitude, N. Longitude, W.	Light above water	Miles seen
	SEACOAST	° ′ ° ′	Feet	
1130	CAPE MAY Fl. W., 30 sec. U.	On cape 38 56.0 74 57.6	165	19
1131	Cape May Radio Direction Finder. Call NSD.	---	---	---

Fig. A1: Light List North Atlantic Coast of the United States, 1939 (pg. 186)

COMDTPUB P16502.2

(1) No.	(2) Name and location	(3) Position	(4) Characteristic	(5) Height	(6) Range	(7) Structure	(8) Remarks
155	Cape May Light	38 56.0 74 57.6	Fl W 15s	165	24	White tower, red lantern, two white dwellings nearby. 170	See pg. xxii for Special Radio Direction Finder Calibration Service

Fig. A2: U.S. Coast Guard Light List, Vol II, 1989 (pg. 2)

30 **Cape May** is the extensive peninsula on the northeast side of the entrance to Delaware Bay. Cape May Light (38°56.0′N., 74°57.6′W.), 165 feet above the water, is shown from a 170-foot white tower on Cape May Point. A special radio direction finder calibration station is at the light. (See Light List for details.)

Fig. A3: United States Coast Pilot #3

85

APPENDIX B

U.S. Lighthouse Administration

1716-1789: First lighthouses erected by Colonies with private monies.

1789-1852: Lighthouses under auspices of an Officer of the U.S. Treasury Department the Fifth Auditor.

1852-1910: Act of Congress creates Lighthouse Board, under the Secretary of the Treasury.

1910-1939: Act of Congress, June 17, 1910, creates Bureau of Lighthouses under the Department of Commerce.

1939-present: President Roosevelt's Reorganization Order Number 2, dated July 1, 1939, consolidates the Bureau of Lighthouses and the U.S. Coast Guard; thus returning lighthouse administration to the Treasury Department.

Administration of the Fifth Auditor

In 1820, the powers within the Treasury Department passed the responsibility for the country's lighthouses to its Fifth Auditor, then Stephen Pleasonton. Mr. Pleasonton had no maritime background, knew nothing of lighthouses, and lacked any semblance of imagination. On the plus side, he was a hard worker, conservative, and tight fisted with government dollars. The department gave this man absolute power over 256 lighthouses, 30 floating lights, a large profusion of beacons and buoys, a legion of personnel, and the safety of U.S. and foreign shipping.

During Pleasonton's 32-year administration, he operated the service with unprecedented economy, saving the government millions of dollars. However, by 1851, when Congress appointed a board to investigate the lighthouse establishment and its operation, this country's lighthouses had fallen far below the standards of the rest of the maritime world. The board's 760-page report found nothing right with the lighthouse system. It detailed an organization with poor management. Most of the lighthouses themselves were too short to be useful and spaced so closely together that seamen couldn't tell them apart. They had been poorly constructed. The personnel, from keepers to maintenance crews, lacked training and morale.

Twenty-nine years had passed since Augustin Fresnel perfected his lens. During that time, his lens had become the standard throughout the world. Pleasonton, who found them to be too expensive, had only installed four of these lenses in the entire United States lighthouse system at the time of the investigation.

Upon receiving the board's report, Congress immediately (October 9, 1852) removed the Fifth Auditor from a position of responsibility and created a nine member Lighthouse Board. The board consisted of members from the Navy, the Corps of Topographical Engineers, the Corps of Army Engineers, the Superintendent of the Coast Survey, and the First Secretary of the Smithsonian Institute. The Secretary of the Treasury served as ex-officio chairman of the board.

One of that board's recommendations called for the construction of several new lighthouse sites and the upgrading of nine important sites: Cape Henlopen, Cape Charles, Cape Henry, Cape Hatteras, Cape Lookout, Cape Fear, Cape Romain, Morris Island (Charleston), and Cape May.

APPENDIX C

Inspection Report, Cape May, June 25, 1851 — 4 p.m.

Sea-coast, revolving. Fifteen reflectors on three faces, ten of them 15-inch parabolic and five of them 14-inch spherical, old and much worn. Downes E. Foster, keeper; 44 years old; carpenter by trade. Light revolves very irregularly — assumed to revolve once in three minutes; no instructions as to time of revolutions; no ventilation, and finds it impossible to keep a good light when the door of the lantern cannot be opened; thin copper below the glass in the lantern; lantern too high, and not of sufficient diameter; cramped for room.

Tower built in 1847, by Samuel Middleton and Nathan Middleton, contractors; tower 78 feet high; keeper took charge April, 1850; removed predecessor; no training or experience before taking charge; no instructions as to the mode of doing the duty; thin plate glass 20 X 28 in the lantern; no paint in dome or frame of lantern — painted black originally; astragals and sashes rusty, and greatly in want of paint; iron conductor; rough square box for leading weight of clock-work movement down; wood-work rough beyond anything seen before; supports to stairway not planed; everything rough and unfinished; tower damp, from base to lantern; a rough hole through the arch of lantern floor for leading weight to clockwork; the whole thing rude in the extreme; cement in this hole good and perfectly hard; tower wants whitewashing outside and in; stairs leading to lantern clean; trims lamp once every night; leaves the light at 9 o'clock and returns at midnight; lights up after sunset, when he thinks it right to do so; extinguishes lights a little before sunrise. Has a copy of written instructions from collector (appointment). Has no printed instructions; never received any. Keeps a tally of oil consumed by lighthouse and dwelling combined; oil always good; received oil from Captain Howland, June 21: summer oil 354 gallons, winter oil 152 gallons; no rule as to the quality or quantity left; no supplies bad; no trimming scissors; no repairs since keeper came here; Captain Howland overhauled lamps, repaired burners, and put in new burners; two spare lamps and burners; does not know when light was inspected, but not since about June, 1850; reported condition of the walls -- need white-washing; has never been supplied with paint or whitewash; no putty; no repairs on buildings except oil-house; no brooms or brushes for cleaning; good water, well out of order; got discouraged at not getting what he asked for, and did not apply any more; cannot tell when the tower was whitewashed inside — outside last spring; burners bad, 7/8 inch; no store-rooms or shelves for wicks, chimneys, tripoli, &c.; summer oil very offensive to the smell; winter oil not so bad, very light color; Howland left two tanks, of bad tin (thin). No journal kept; makes returns once a quarter in the usual form; collector at Wilmington, Del., is the superintendent. Dwelling built in September, 1847; leaks through the walls in a stream; rain drives in at the windows; plastering broken; whitewashed three weeks since; windows loose; oil consumed last year for house and lamps, 449 gallons; (evidently a bad light, and great want of ventilation); Howland wanted to know what had been done with the oil over and above the quantity used by the keeper; Captain H. sounds the oil-tanks, determines what is on hand, and leaves what quantity he pleases; keeper receipts for the quantity he says he leaves; has no means of ascertaining the quantity; does not know how much the tanks hold; Captain Howland remains less than half a day, usually; no clock allowed; finds his own time-piece.

  This is a boat-station for wrecks. Boat-house locked; keeper has not charge of it; it is in charge of a person not far off; called on the keeper of the wrecking apparatus and examined it.

APPENDIX D

Fourth District Engineers Report, 20 March 1878

CAPE MAY

On north side of entrance to Delaware Bay, Lower Township, Cape May County, New Jersey, in 38° 55' 50" north latitude and 74° 57' 36" west longitude.

Is reached by West Jersey Railroad from Philadelphia to Cape May City, 81 miles, thence by private conveyance 3 miles to the lighthouse; or during the summer season by steamboat from Philadelphia to Sea Grove. The station being on the outskirts of that summer resort, hotels are to be found in the immediate vicinity.

TOWER

The tower is of brick, the watch-room gallery being 145 feet above the base; cement-washed gray.

It is on masonry 12 feet deep laid on a grillage 12 inches deep, and has an exterior conical wall 3 feet 9 inches in thickness at the bottom, with an outside diameter of 27 feet. At the top the wall has a thickness of 1 foot 6 inches, with an exterior diameter of 13 feet 6 inches, and an interior cylindrical 9-inch wall with an inside diameter of 10 feet 6 inches, through which passes a cast-iron spiral stairway to watch-room. The tower is entered through a two-story vestibule; the first floor of which is divided into passage into tower, with oil-room on each side, the second floor into 1 storeroom.

The lens is of the 1st order, by Henry Lepaute, flashing every 30 seconds, and illuminating the entire horizon, and is supplied with 3 hydraulic lamps and has 16 flash-panels.
The focal plane is 167 feet above the mean level of the sea.

DWELLINGS

There are two keeper's dwellings; the foundation and cellar walls are of brick, and buildings are frame, lathed and plastered inside, one and a half stories high; 1st story is divided into 3 rooms and entry with stairway, porch in front, and inclosed shed over back door; the second floors are divided into 4 rooms. There are cellars under each house, paved with brick; the buildings are well supplied with closets throughout; there is one well between the houses, and no cistern.

The present tower and buildings were erected by mechanics and laborers employed and paid in part by the day and in part by the month; commenced under the direction of Captain (now Lieutenant Colonel) William F. Raynolds, continued by Captain W.B. Franklin, and finished by the late Major Bache, all of the Corps of Engineers, U.S.A. Tower finished 1859; dwellings finished in 1860.

SITE

The deeds for this site bear dates: No. 1, of April 9th 1847; No. 2, April 8th 1858, and are from Alexander Whilldin and wife, to the United States; the consideration for the first being $1,150 and for the second being $500, and they are described as follows: No. 1. "Beginning at a red cedar post standing on the fast land near the edge of the marsh and slough on the easterly side of the point of said Great Island, and running from thence N. 65° W.12 perches and 12 links to red cedar post standing back in the field, which said post in the field is the north-westerly corner of said lot herein mentioned and intended to be conveyed, and from which post, by the present position of the compass, the spire or top of the steeple on the Presbyterian church on Cape May Island bears N. 88° 30' E., and the top of the chimney on the westerly end of said Alexander Whilldin's new farm-house bears N. 5° E.; and from thence S 25°W. 26 perches to a red cedar post; from thence S. 65° E. 12 perches and 12 links to a red cedar post standing on the fast land near the marsh and slough from thence N. 25° E. 26 perches to the first place of beginning; within which bounds are contained 2 acres of land, be the same more or less."

No. 2. "All that lot of land situate on an island near the point of Cape May, commonly called Great Island, in the Lower Township of the County of Cape May and State of New Jersey, butted

Appendix D - Fourth District Engineer's Report, 1878

and bounded as follows: Beginning at a stone for a corner standing in a line along the west side of a lot of land formerly conveyed by the said parties of the first part to the said parties of the second, and which said stone is distant 1 chain 51 links from the northwest corner of said last-mentioned lot, and running thence N 22° W. 9 chains and 56 links to a stone for a corner; thence N.68° E. 2 chains and 20 links to another stone for a corner; thence S. 22° E. 9 chains 76 links to another stone for a corner, to the line of the northerly side of said lot formerly conveyed as aforesaid to the party of the second part; thence along said line N. 65° 10' W. 1 chain 65 links to a stone; thence along the westerly line of said last-mentioned tract S. 24° 50' W. 1 chain 51 links to the place of beginning; within which bounds are contained 2 acres, be the same more or less."

The lot is level and arable, about 3 acres being under cultivation. About 8 feet of the base of the tower of 1847 was left standing when the tower was removed; it is roofed over and serves for a store-house; the keeper's old dwelling is used for a stable and barn.

The station was first established in 1823; the approximate position of the original is shown on the map; it is now some 100 yards from the shore. At the time of the erection of the tower of 1847 the high-water line had surrounded the old tower.

The site conveyed for this lighthouse was from John Stites and wife, to the United States, the consideration being $300, and the amount of land 1 acre.

The house and appliances of the life-saving station exhibited at the Centennial Exhibition has since been erected on the southerly end of lot No. 1.

Within the past 3 years a summer watering-place, "Sea Grove," has grown up on Cape May, in the immediate vicinity of the lighthouse, and during the summer season is quite a thriving town, patronized chiefly by members of the Presbyterian Church.

There are three keepers.

APPENDIX E
Map of Cape May Point Showing Erosion

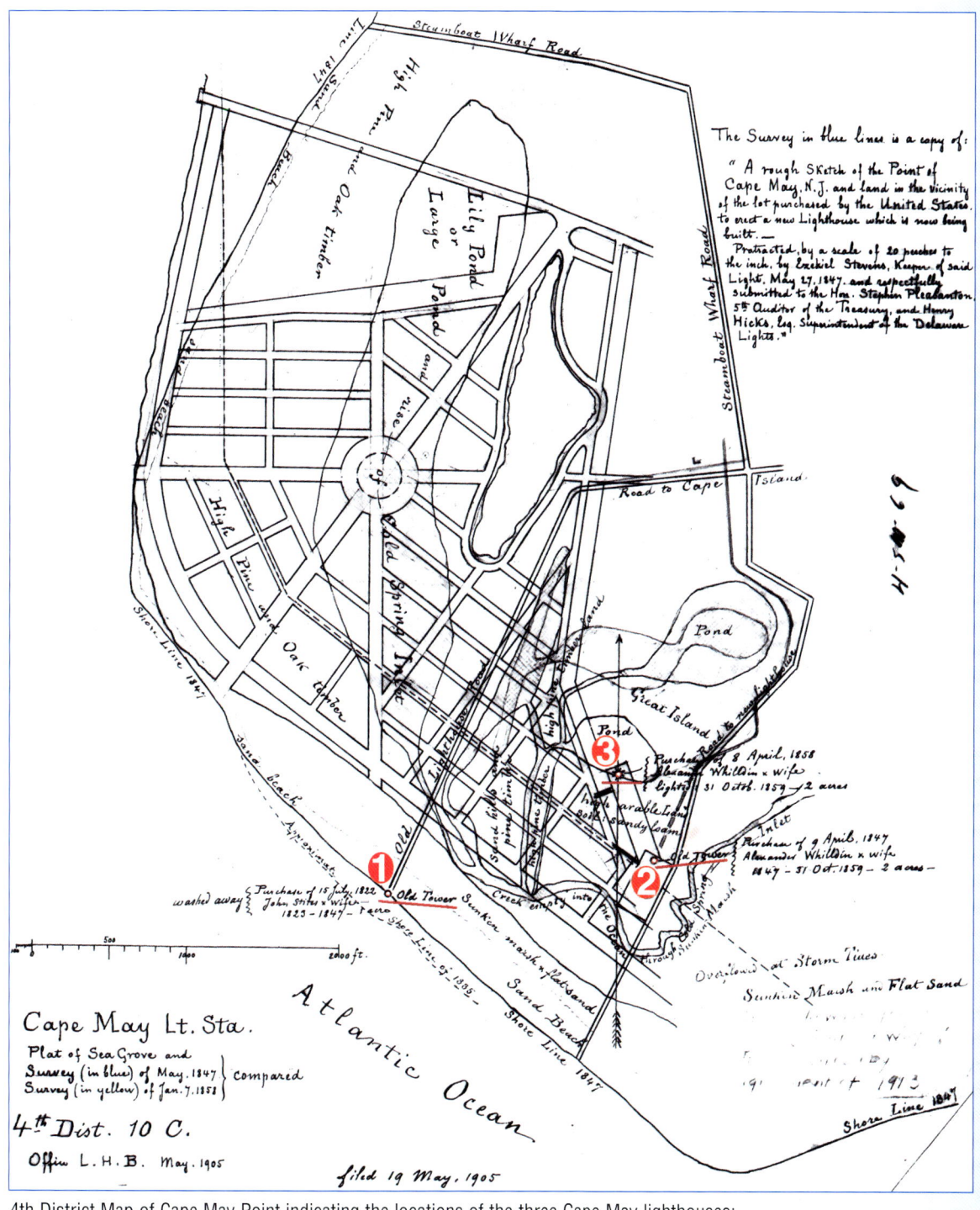

4th District Map of Cape May Point indicating the locations of the three Cape May lighthouses:
1 = 1823 lighthouse **2** = 1847 lighthouse **3** = 1859 lighthouse (the present location)

APPENDIX F

Keepers[39]

Keeper	Assistant Keeper	Salary	Date of Appointment	Date of Vacation	How Vacated
Ephraim Mills[40]	None	unknown	unknown, prob. 1823	unknown	Unknown
Ezekiel Stevens	None	unknown	unknown, prob. 1823-28	April 1850	Removed[41]
Downes E. Foster	None	unknown	April 1850	Sept. 22, 1853	Unknown
William C. Gregory	None	400.	Sept. 22, 1853	Mar. 26, 1861	Unknown
	Samuel Stillwell (1)[1]	250	Sept. 14, 1859	Oct. 18, 1861	Promoted
	John Reeves (2)	250	Sept. 14, 1859	Jul. 6, 1860	
	J. Belanger (2)	250	July 6, 1860	Oct. 18, 1861	
Downes E. Foster		720	Mar. 26, 1861	Sept. 4, 1879	Removed
	Reuben Foster (2)	250	Oct. 18, 1861	Sept. 4, 1862	Unknown
	Sam L. Foster (1)	250	Oct. 18, 1861	Jan.13, 1866	
	Douglas Foster (2)	250	Sept. 4, 1862	Oct. 12, 1867	
	L. Cumings (1)	250	Jan 13, 1866	Mar. 30, 1866	
	Jacob A. Snyder (1)	350	Mar. 30, 1866	Oct. 12, 1867	Appt 2d asst
	William Henderson (1)	400	Dec. 14, 1866	Apr. 1, 1873	Appt 2d asst
	J. A. Snyder (2)	400	Oct. 12, 1867	Mar. 24, 1869	Resigned
	A.E.D. Crowell (2)	400	Mar. 24, 1869	Apr. 5, 1873	Resigned
	Geo. W. Everingham(1)	400	Apr 3, 1873	May 3, 1873	Appt 2d asst
	Geo. W. Everingham(2)	390	May 3, 1873	Apr. 3,1876	Promoted
	William Henderson (2)	390	Apr. 1, 1873	May 3, 1873	Promoted
	William Henderson (1)	400	May 3, 1873	Apr. 3, 1877	Resigned
	Lewis D. Stevens (2)	390	Apr. 3, 1876	Oct. 9, 1877	Promoted
	George W. Everingham (1)	400	Apr. 3, 1876	Oct. 9, 1877	Resigned
Samuel Stillwell (acting keeper)		700	Oct. 9, 1877	Sept. 9, 1878	Per Appt.
	Lewis D. Stevens (acting 1)	400	Oct. 9, 1877	Sept. 9, 1878	Per Appt.
	Howard Stites (acting 2)	390	Oct. 9, 1877	Sept 9, 1878	Per Appt.

Keeper	Assistant Keeper	Salary	Date of Appointment	Date of Vacation	How Vacated
Samuel Stillwell		700	Sept. 9, 1878	Oct. 1, 1903[42]	Retired
	Lewis D. Stevens (1)	400	Sept. 9, 1878	Dec. 10, 1880	Removed
	Howard Stiles (2)	390	Sept. 9, 1878	Aug. 11, 1881	Transferred
	Wm. B. Eldredge (actg 1)	400	Jan. 10, 1881	Aug. 20, 1881	Perm. Appt.
	William B. Eldredge (1)	400	Aug. 20, 1881	May 16, 1882	Resigned
	Enos Edmonds (acting 2)	390	Sept. 9, 1881	Dec. 15, 1881	Perm. Appt.
	Enos Edmunds (2)	390	Dec. 15, 1881	May 16, 1882	Promoted
	Lewis G. Eldridge (acting 2)	390	May 16, 1882	July 7, 1882	Perm. Appt.
	Enos Edmunds (acting 1)	400	May 16, 1882	Feb. 27, 1883	Resigned
	Lewis G. Eldridge (2)	390	July 7, 1882	Feb. 27, 1883	Promoted
	Lewis G. Eldridge (acting 1)	400	Feb. 27, 1883	Apr. 30, 1883	Perm. Appt.
	Caleb Woolson (acting 2)	390	Mar. 1, 1883	Apr 30, 1883	Perm. Appt
	Lewis G. Eldridge (1)	400	Apr. 30, 1883	May 14, 1892	Removed
	Caleb Swain Woolson (2)	390	Apr. 30, 1883	May 19, 1892	Pro-moted
	Caleb S. Woolson (1)	480	May 19, 1892	Oct. 1, 1903	Promoted
	Edward Hughes (acting 2)	460	June 10, 1892	Apr. 22, 1893	Absolute
	Edward Hughes (2)	460	Apr. 22, 1893	Oct. 1, 1903	Promoted
Caleb S. Woolson		760	Oct. 1, 1903	May 1924	
	Edward Hughes (1)	480	Oct. 1, 1903	May 1924	
	Jno. S. Pusey(2)	460	Oct. 1, 1903	Apr. 1, 1906	
	Elwood E. Benstead(2)	460	Apr. 1, 1906	May 1924	Retired on disability
Harry H. Palmer		960	May 1924	July 1, 1933	Retired
	Edwin Wilson (1)		May 1924	1933 (u)[2]	
	Floyd K. Schmierer (1)		1927 (u)	1933 (u)	
	Otis James Franklin Williams(2)	May 1924 (u)	1926 (u)		

1-Assistant keepers: (1) First Assistant, (2) Second Assistant. After 1918 all assistant keepers were called simply keepers.
2 - (u) Undocumented. Information gathered from speaking with descendants of the keepers who remember the person being on site.

APPENDIX G

Historical Name

*E*ver since that time in 1986 when MAC tried to change the name of this lighthouse to the "Cape May Point Lighthouse," confusion has reigned regarding its real name. Is it the Cape May Lighthouse or the Cape May Point Lighthouse? Please feel free to call it whatever you wish. However, the Lighthouse Service names lighthouses for the geographic land masses or waterways that they mark for mariners. This lighthouse marks the geographic peninsula of Cape May, so it is the Cape May Lighthouse. Lighthouses rarely mark cities or towns. For example, the Key West Lighthouse marks the island of Key West, not the town of Key West. The Absecon Lighthouse marks the Absecon Inlet, not Atlantic City. Please remember that, at the time that this lighthouse station was established (1823), not only was Cape May Point not incorporated, but Lower Township, Cape May City and anything else around here was not incorporated. Cape May City was Cape Island. I include a listing of official and unofficial documents that reference the lighthouse for your information and amusement:

Letter from Lieut. T. A. Jenkins to the Coast Survey Office, Washington City, DC, urging "no delay in upgrading the following Lighthouses..." November 5, 1851 "12. Cape May, revolving light."

U.S. Lighthouse Board Preliminary Report, recommending a taller lighthouse for the site, January 30, 1852 "Cape May."

U.S. Lighthouse Service Annual Report, 1853, Pg. 196 "Capes May and Henlopen."

U.S. Lighthouse Service Annual Report, 1857 "Cape May."

U.S. Lighthouse Service Annual Report, 1858 "Cape May lighthouse."

Scheyichbi and the Strand, Edward S. Wheeler, 1876, Pg. 94, "Cape May Lighthouse."

Fourth District Engineers Report, March 20, 1878 "Cape May."

Cape May Star & Wave, March 8, 1879, Pg. 3 "Cape May Light House."

Cape May Star & Wave, June 21, 1884, Pg. 3 "Cape May Light House."

U.S. Lighthouse Service Annual Report, 1884, 253 "Cape May, at Cape May Point..."

Fourth District Engineers Survey of the Station, 1886 "Cape May Light Station."

Document of Appropriations, U.S. government form 152, 1822-1862 "Cape May light-station."

Annual Report of the Lighthouse Board to the Secretary of the Treasury for the Fiscal Year ended June 30, 1888 (on map) "Cape May Light."

Captioned photographs, taken from offshore, enclosed with the U.S. Lighthouse Service Annual Reports: 1892, 1895, and 1900 "Cape May Light-Station."

Head of form fill-in space (hand written) on ledger pages listing keepers' salaries 1901 and 1905 "Name of Light Station: Cape May, NJ."

Cape May Herald, 1902 "Cape May Point Lighthouse."

Cape May Herald, 1903 "Cape May Lighthouse."

Fourth District Engineers Erosion survey, based on a drawing by keeper Ezekial Stevens (1823) and surveys taken in 1847 and 1858, filed May 19, 1905 "Cape May Lt. Sta."

Letter to Harry Palmer from G. W. Hitchens, Acting 4th District Supt., USLHS, June 12, 1933 "Cape May Light Station."

New York Times, "New Light for Cape May, Sec. III," Pg. 10, Aug. 19, 1934 "Cape May Light."

New York Times, "New Beacons Being Tried, Sec. III," Pg. 10, Sept. 30, 1934 "Cape May Lighthouse."

Letter to Mrs. H. H. Palmer from N. C. Manyon, 4th District Supt., USLHS, November 1, 1935 "Custodian, Cape May Light Station."

United States Coast Pilot 3, Atlantic Coast: Sandy Hook to Cape Henry, 1987 "Cape May Light."

CCGD5 Aids Work Report (Coast Guard routine maintenance report form), March, 1988, "545 Cape May Lt."

U. S. Coast Guard Light List, Vol II, Atlantic Coast: Toms River, New Jersey to Little River, South Carolina, 1989, Pg. 2 "Cape May Light."

Rand McNally Road Atlas, United States, Canada, Mexico, 1998, Pg. 63 "Cape May Light-house."

The Press of Atlantic City, Friday, May 8, 1998, Region (Section C), "Cape May Lighthouse name of choice in The Press poll," Richard Degener.

APPENDIX H

A Chronology of Lighthouses

660 BCE   Lesches, a Greek poet, tells of a lighthouse on Sigaeum in the Troad (area of Troy). This may be the first regularly operated lighthouse in the world. Its location would have guided ships to Troy, Hellespoint, the Sea of Marmora, the Bosphorus, and the Black Sea.

292 BCE   Colossus of Rhodes (one of the seven wonders of the ancient world), a 70 cubit (105 ft) bronze statue of Apollo. Sculpted by a pupil of the Great Greek sculptor Lysippus, it stood at the entrance to the harbor of Rhodes and supposedly held a torch aloft, much like our present day Statue of Liberty, upon which they built a fire at night to guide mariners into the harbor. The Colossus lasted 500 years, finally broken off at the knee and toppled in an earthquake in 225 AD.

280 BCE   Pharos of Alexandria (another one of the seven wonders of the ancient world), the first known lighthouse and the tallest ever built approximately 450 ft. tall. Its Egyptian builder inscribed on the finished structure, "Sostratus of Gnidus, son of Dixiphanus, to the Gods protecting those upon the sea." It lasted 1500 years and travelers reported it still standing in the 12th century. An earthquake finally toppled it. This lighthouse became so renowned that the word Pharos evolved to mean sea lights in languages throughout the world. Today, pharology means the science of lighthouse engineering .

Pre-75 BCE   The Lighthouse at Messina, guarding the dangerous whirlpool of Carybdis, as depicted on a coin produced by Sextus Pompeius (75-35 BCE) has the distinction of being considered the oldest of the Roman lighthouses in Italy.

               Julius Caesar (100-44 BCE) makes repairs to the Roman lighthouse of La Coruna at Julio Briga, Spain. It has been altered several times over the years with the last major alteration in 1790. Once known as the Column (or Pillar) of Hercules, La Coruna has the distinction of being the worlds oldest operational lighthouse.[43]

50 BCE   The Roman ports of Ostia (port of Rome), Ravenna, and Puteoli have lighthouses to guide commerce into their harbors.

40 AD   Emperor Caligula builds a lighthouse near present day Boulogne, France, an octagonal tower , 192 feet in circumference, about 64 feet in diameter and from 124 to 200 feet in height (depending on the era and historian quoted). He builds it along the lines of most Roman lighthouses with 12 stories, each 1 ½ feet narrower than the story immediately below forming a pyramid shape. It will last until the 17th century.

400   The Roman Empire has over 30 lighthouses in service from the Black Sea to the Atlantic.

1460 (est)	Christopher Columbus' uncle becomes keeper of the Genoa Lighthouse. Young Christopher and his parents visit and stay with his uncle every summer. Could it be that young Christopher sites a ship on the horizon that disappears when he descends the tower, and reappears when he climbs the tower? It could be where he discovered that the world was round. We could draw from this that his lighthouse experience ultimately sent him on his quest to discover America.[44]
1665	Sir Robert Reading receives a patent to build private lighthouses in Ireland. He builds several "Brazier Lighthouses" in that country. Brazier Lighthouses consist of a stone-vaulted keeper's cottage containing stone stairs leading up to a small platform on the roof. The keeper kept an open fire, of coal, wood, or peat, burning upon this platform.[45]
1716	The Massachusetts Bay Colony builds the first lighthouse in America, the Boston Lighthouse.
1781	Aimé Argand, Swiss scientist, invents a lamp for lighthouses with a hollow wick that burns brightly and smokelessly. Oxygen flows both inside and outside of the burning wick producing a light equal to the light of seven candles.
1783	M. Teulere, French Engineer, develops catoptric light system combining parabolic reflectors and Argand lamps.
1789	Aug. 7, U.S. Lighthouse Service established under the Treasury Department. It is the ninth law enacted by the first congress, signed by President George Washington, August 7th. It provides that the lighthouses should be under the supervision of the Secretary of the Treasury. Sept. 11, Alexander Hamilton appointed Secretary of the Treasury. He assumes immediate supervision of the lighthouses of the United States. (Interestingly, Congress hadn't provided for a Treasury Department until the next day.) Sept. 12, Congress passes an act providing for a Treasury Department.
1790	June 18, Alexander Hamilton, Secretary of the Treasury, presents his official report on the nation's lighthouses to President Washington. It is the first official report on U.S. lighthouses.[46] Aug. 4, First Congress establishes the U.S. Revenue Marine, later known as the Revenue Cutter Service. It will become the Coast Guard when consolidated with the Lifesaving Service in 1915.
1810	Captain Winslow Lewis patents the Argand Lamp and Teulere parabolic reflector system

Appendix H - A Chronology of Lighthouses

	in this country for lighting U.S. lighthouses. He receives $60,000 for the patent and a government contract to furnish lamps and supplies for all federal lighthouses for $27,000 per year.
1812	Lewis' system receives approval for installation in the nation's lighthouses.
1822	Augustin Fresnel perfects his lens that will revolutionize the lighting of lighthouses.
1848	Congress appropriates $10,000 for the purpose of placing lifesaving equipment along the New Jersey coast. Designed to save lives, the government locates them near lighthouses, so that lighthouse keepers along with volunteers can man them.
1851	Congress appoints investigating board to inspect the country's lighthouse establishment.
1852	*Jan. 30*, Lighthouse Board reports to Congress on a lighthouse establishment in a shambles. It calls for the upgrading of nine important seacoast lighthouses: Cape Charles (VA), Cape Fear (NC), Cape Hatteras (NC), Cape Henlopen (DE), Cape Henry (VA), Cape Lookout (NC), Cape Romain (SC), Cape May (NJ), and Morris Island, (SC). Congress creates Lighthouse Board under the Secretary of the Treasury.
1855	Sperm whale oil, the fuel of lighthouse lamps becomes scarce. Its price rises to $2.25 per gallon. The service experiments with dolphin, lard, and colzan oils as replacements.
1886	*Oct. 28*, President Grover Cleveland dedicates the Statue of Liberty, a gift from the people of France, in New York Harbor. The Lighthouse Service uses the torch as a channel marker for the harbor.
1871	The chief of the Revenue Cutter Service, Sumner I. Kimball, establishes a modern lifesaving organization. Professional surf men man the lifesaving stations. They patrol the beaches during darkness and heavy weather.
1878	Kerosene introduced as the fuel of lighthouses. U.S. Lifesaving Service organizes as separate from the Revenue Cutter Service under the Treasury Department.
1900	Electricity first tested as light source in lighthouses.
1915	*Jan. 28*, U.S. Coast Guard created by consolidating the Revenue Cutter Service and the Lifesaving Service.
1918	Bureau of Lighthouses changes title of District Inspector to Superintendent.
1920	Bureau of Lighthouses converts majority of country's lighthouses to electricity.
1939	U.S. Coast Guard and Lighthouse Service consolidated.

1828 Letter of Recommendation

A letter to Congressman Thomas Senneckson, Esq. recommending the appointment of Mr. Joseph Anniss as keeper of the first Cape May lighthouse. Notice the recommended qualifications! To the best of our knowledge, Mr. Anniss was not appointed.

Mount Holly 27th November 1828

Thomas Senneckson, Esq.

Sir - It is understood that a Light House is erected at Cape May and that it will be necessary to apoint a suitable person as Keeper -- I do not know whether the appointment is to be made by the President or his Navy appointment -- My object at this time is respectfully to recommend to your notice Mr. Joseph Anniss of the County of Somerset -- He is a gentleman of unblemished character in his decline of life and in rather indigent circumstances but amply qualified to the faithful discharge of the duties of any office he would solicit -- He now holds the appointment of a Judge of the Pleas and has for many years represented his County in the Legislature.

Mr. Anniss is desirous to obtain from the general government the appointment of Keeper of this Light House and in order to his success it will be proper that he should procure the recommendation of the members of the Congress from this State. Mr. Anniss was a Whig of seventy-six -- and has always been an understanding Federalist of the old Washington school and is now in favor of the present administration. He is in my opinion amply qualified for this appointment and I beg leave to refer you to the Honorable Lewis Condit, one of our members of Congress, for the character and standing of Judge Anniss -- to whom he is personally known -- If Sir upon inquiry into the character of Mr. A you can consistent with your ideas of propriety join with the other members of Congress in recommending him to the proper source for this appointment you will confer a favor on a worthy man. I hope Sir you will excuse the liberty I have taken in thus addressing you -- my only object is to recommend an old and much esteemed friend -- and one who if appointed will do justice to all concerned.

I am Sir with much respect
Your Obed. Serv.

Thos Senneckson   Saml. J. Read

101

APPENDIX I

Lighthouses of New Jersey and the Delaware Bay (In order of establishment date)

Sandy Hook, NJ, 1764, 3rd order, height 85', fp 103'47 octagonal brick tower, white with red lantern. The oldest continuously operating lighthouse in the country, built by Colonial New York businessmen through a lottery. (It is the only Colonial lighthouse to survive through to present times.) During the Revolution before the expected arrival of the British Fleet, the New York Congress decided to "render the lighthouse entirely useless" to the British. They removed the lamps and oil, but the tower remained. Lieutenant Colonel Benjamin Tupper ordered his soldiers to destroy the tower. They played artillery directly into the tower walls for over an hour, but found the walls so firm that they could "make no impression." After the skirmish, the Americans left Sandy Hook in British hands. Tower not open to the public. Located in the Fort Hancock Historical museum, Gateway National Recreation area, Sandy Hook, NJ, 201-872-0115.

Cape Henlopen, DE, 1776, The tower was 26 feet in diameter, 6 feet thick at the base, 69 feet, 3 inches tall, and 17 feet, 6 inches in diameter and 3 feet thick at the top. It was built by the Pennsylvania Board of Port Wardens on the north side of the Great Dune, 46 feet above sea level, to obtain additional height. During the Revolution, British troops burned the tower. The colonists rebuilt it in 1784 only to have it burned again by the French in 1812. They rebuilt it this time with fire-proof iron stairs. Erosion undermined its dune and it toppled from its lofty perch and fell onto the beach in a severe storm April 13, 1926. Many of Lewes' fine homes built around that time contain bricks from the tower.

Ship John Shoal, NJ, 1798 (approx.), 1877, This lighthouse marks the shoal named after the square rigger, John, that grounded on the shoal in the early winter of 1797. By spring the heavy ice had cut through the hull and it gradually settled into the sand. Drifting sand accumulated around the wreck creating a large shoal. A wooden light structure marked the shoal soon after the John's disaster. The treacherous bay ice destroyed that structure by 1876. The government ordered a new caisson lighthouse for the site. The newly completed lighthouse went first to the nation's Centennial exhibition and spent its first year as the centerpiece for the Lighthouse Service exhibit.

Cape Henlopen lying on the beach moments after toppling April 13, 1926. Photo from the collection of John Bailey.

Its caisson stood empty in the bay that year waiting to receive its lighthouse. In 1877, workers dismantled the lighthouse, shipped it here, and placed it on its waiting caisson base. It is a 65-foot tower surmounted by a light visible for 13 miles. Thirty-seven hundred tons of stone rip-rap surrounds the lighthouse for protection from the ice. The lighthouse features a charming mansard roof with dormer windows and eyebrow windows and vents surmounted by a bell-roofed cupola with a catwalk. One of the souvenirs at the lighthouse is the wooden figurehead of the ship, *John*. It is located in the bay and not open to visitors.

Cape May, NJ, 1823, 1847, 1859, 1st order, hgt 157.5', fp 175' round brick tower, cream with red lantern. The second oldest continuously operating lighthouse in the country, built by Corps of Engineers. First use of sodium vapor lamp in a lighthouse, 1934. Located in the Cape May Point State Park. Tower and museum shop, open to the public, maintained and operated by the Mid-Atlantic Center for the Arts (MAC), 609-884-5404.

Appendix I - Lighthouses of New Jersey and the Delaware Bay

Ship John Shoal Lighthouse. Photo from the collection of John Bailey.

Brandywine Light Station. Official U.S. Coast Guard photo.

Brandywine Shoal, NJ, 1827, 1848, 1914, Originally a lightship marked this shoal but the winter ice continually forced the ship off station. The government built a lighthouse here in 1827 but the drifting ice floes of the bay destroyed it within 12 months and a lightship again took up station marking the shoal until 1850. In 1848 workers began building the first screwpile lighthouse in the U.S. on the site. They screwed nine spidery legs 22 feet into the bottom and surrounded them with an ice-breaking fence. It lasted 60 years. In 1914 the present lighthouse replaced the old screw-pile. It is the first caisson type of structure built in the U.S. The caisson is a 35 foot diameter cylinder, built in Lewes, Delaware, floated out and sunk on the shoal. It is filled with concrete and surrounded with rip rap for ice protection. It was the last Delaware Bay Lighthouse with a resident keeper, automated in 1974. The Coast Guard conducted a thorough reconstruction and restoration of

Brandywine Shoal in 1987. Located in the bay off of Cape May, it is not open to the public.

Twin Towers of Navesink, NJ, 1828, 1862, 1st order, height 73', fp 256' military fortress structure of field stone with two lighthouse towers, one at each end, and built on a high bluff. The first Fresnel lenses in the U.S. were installed at Twin Lights, 1840. (Commander Matthew C. Perry brought the first two lenses into the U.S. for Navesink.) The first use of kerosene in a U.S. First-Order lighthouse, 1883. The first electrically powered primary light in the U.S., 1898. (Harbor lights were already using electricity; but the early bulbs were not bright enough for First-Order seacoast lights.) The first wireless telegraph message was transmitted by Guglielmo Marconi from the Great White Fleet honoring Dewey. A telegraph operator at Twin Lights received the message. The most powerful light in the U.S., the electric arc and bi-valve lens- 25 million-candlepower lamp, was installed at Navesink in 1920. It was cut back to 9 million candlepower in 1931. Towers, lighthouse museum, Lifesaving Service museum, and museum shop open to the public. Located off Route 36, Highlands, NJ, 201-872-1814.

Navesink. Photo from the collection of John Bailey.

Barnegat Inlet, NJ, 1835, 1859, 1st order, height 161', fp 175' round brick tower, upper half red, lower half white. Original lens on display at the nearby Barnegat Light Historical Museum. Built by corps of Engineers and believed to have been designed by Capt. George G. Meade. Located at Barnegat Lighthouse State Park, Barnegat Light (northernmost tip of Long Beach Island), NJ, 609-494-2016.

Harbor of Refuge (South), DE, 1839, 1926, In the early 1800s mariners petitioned the government to build a harbor where their ships could find safety behind Cape Henlopen during severe weather. In 1825, Congress authorized the construction of a breakwater and an icebreaker pier. Workers completed construction in 1839 and placed a lighthouse, the

Appendix I - Lighthouses of New Jersey and Delaware Bay

Harbor of Refuge Lighthouse (1925) in the shipyard ready to be towed to the site. Photo from the collection of John Bailey.

East Point Lighthouse.
Photo: Cape Publishing, Inc.

Harbor of Refuge Lighthouse at the west end of the breakwater to mark the entrance to the harbor. In 1920 a storm badly damaged the lighthouse and it was replaced in 1926 to take over the duties of the fallen Cape Henlopen Lighthouse. It is white with a black lantern.

Absecon Inlet, NJ, 1856, 1st order, height 171', fp 167' round brick tower, white with red band around middle, red lantern. The lighthouse marks Absecon Inlet. Like the Cape May and Barnegat Lighthouses, Capt. Meade probably designed this one. It became so surrounded by tall buildings that its light could no longer reach the open ocean. The government placed a beacon on the boardwalk, decommissioned the light in 1932, and turned it over to the state of New Jersey. The Inlet Public/Private Association completed a two-year, $3.5 million restoration project in October, 1999 and celebrated by relighting the lighthouse. The restoration effort was marred by an arsonist who destroyed the partially built copy of the Keeper's cottage. The cottage was rebuilt and is to become a visitor's orientation center and museum. Plans are to open the tower to the public. Located at Pacific & Rhode Island Aves., Atlantic City, NJ.

East Point, NJ, 1857, 4th order, 2-story brick structure painted white. Originally named the Maurice (pronounced Morris) River Lighthouse, it marks the entrance to the Maurice River. One of three lights that marked the approaches to the River, (see Egg Island, N.J. 1898) this one guided mariners past Dead Man's Shoal and into the entrance channel, an area of intense ship and boat-building, and shellfish harvesting until the 1940s. The building's design is the same as many early west coast lighthouses such as Battery Point (1856) and Point Loma (1891). It has a fireplace in each room, but had no plumbing, electricity or heat. Kerosene fueled the light and household lamps. A cistern collected rainwater that ran from the roof for cooking, washing, and drinking. The government decommissioned it and extinguished the light in 1941. A trespasser's discarded cigarette started a fire in the abandoned lighthouse that destroyed the original cast iron cupola, the roof, the second floor and the attic. In 1972, tropical storm Agnes knocked down the chimney and gable end. That same year, the Maurice River Historical Society received permission to restore and rebuild the lighthouse. The Coast Guard reactivated the lighthouse in July of 1980 and installed an automated beacon in the rebuilt cupola which faithfully replicates the original. Mariners can see the light for 10 miles across the bay. A caretakers cottage, completed in 1984 and occupied since, has decreased the vandalism significantly. Located south of Heislerville. No regular visitor's hours. 609-825-3386.

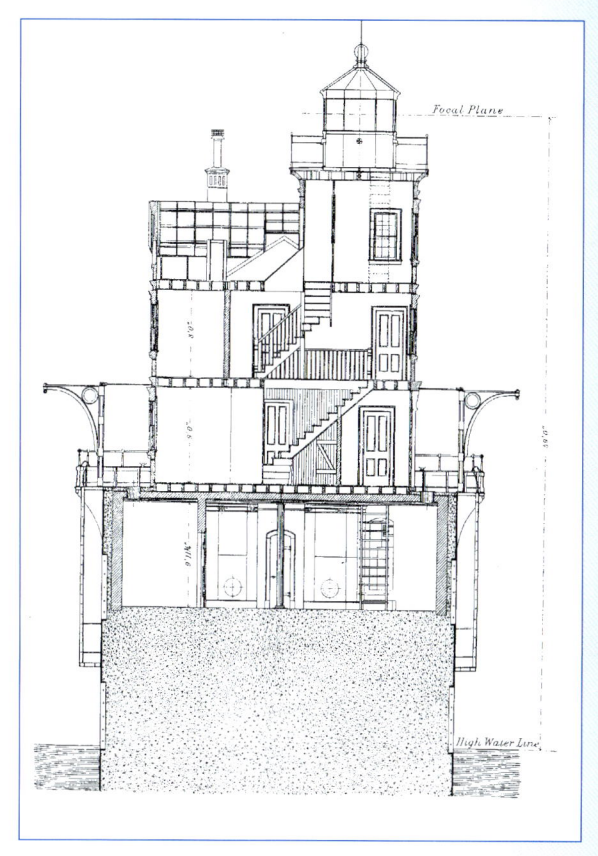

Fourteen Foot Bank cutaway drawing. Illustration Official U.S. Lighthouse Service diagram.

Hereford Inlet, NJ, 1874, 4th order, height 49.5' fp 53', frame clapboard building, white with red lantern. In 1871 the Lifesaving Service built a U.S. Lifesaving Station (#36) in the small fishing village of Anglesea (now North Wildwood) at the northern tip of Five Mile Beach on Hereford Inlet. The lighthouse followed it three years later and marks the inlet for fishing boats. The station hosted the first religious service on the island when the third keeper, Freeling Hewett, gathered the fishermen's families together in the lighthouse parlor and conducted a Baptist service there. A severe storm undermined the lighthouse's foundation in August 1913, forcing the lighthouse to be moved westward about 150 feet where it stands today. It served as an active light until replaced by an automatic beacon in 1964. Then went back into commission in April 1986 and serves as an active navigational

Appendix I - Lighthouses of New Jersey and Delaware Bay

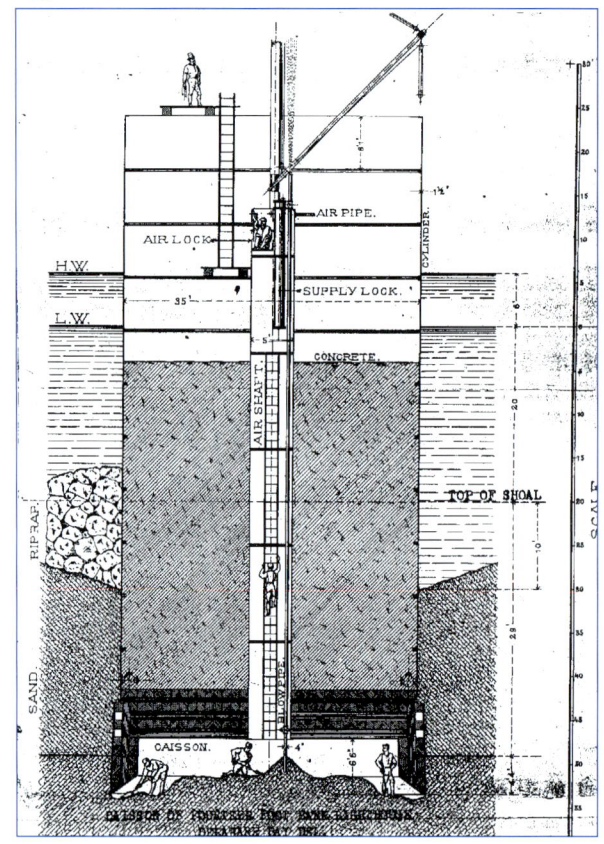

Workers sinking caisson for Fourteen Foot Bank Light Station. Official U.S. Lighthouse Service diagram.

aid today. The National Park Service placed it on the National Register of Historic Places on Sept. 20,1977. Museum and information center open June thru September. Located at 1st and Central Aves. North Wildwood, NJ 08260, 609-522-4520.

Fourteen Foot Bank, DE, 1886, Like Brandywine Shoal, a lightship originally marked this shallow bank, followed by a screwpile structure. Then in 1886, after the ice had taken its toll, this caisson replaced the damaged screwpile. Workers also built this caisson ashore, floated it out to the sight then sank it into the sandy bottom using a pneumatic process and filled it with concrete. This is the first lighthouse in the U.S. to be built on a submarine foundation. The 1901 Light List describes the structure as a "cylindrical foundation expanding in trumpet shape under a main gallery, surmounted by a 2-story dwelling with a gable roof; tower surmounted by lantern rises from easterly side of dwelling... entire structure, brown. The color scheme has been changed to white with a black lantern. Located in the bay. Not open to the public.

Statue of Liberty, NJ, 1886, a gift from France, dedicated Oct. 28, 1886, the government turned the statue over to the Lighthouse Board on Nov. 22. The board had the metal sides of the torch cut away, installed glass, a lamp, and a lens. It had its own electric plant on the island (then called Bedloe). It served as an active harbor light until March 1, 1902, althought ship's navigators continued to use it as a marker.

Breakwater, DE, 1885, 1926, in order to provide greater safety for vessels in the Harbor of Refuge, the government closed the gap between the breakwater and the icebreaker pier

Egg Island Lighthouse keepers' dwelling. Postcard from the collection of John Bailey.

and placed a lighthouse at the east end of it in 1885. It was a brown conical tower 56 feet tall. In 1896, Congress authorized another expansion of the Harbor of Refuge adding a new breakwater and several icebreaker piers. They marked the entrance to the harbor by placing a lighthouse on the south end of the breakwater. A storm damaged this lighthouse beyond repair, so the service replaced it in 1926 with the present lighthouse. It is a brown lighthouse on a white pier, with a black lantern holding a 4th order light 61 feet above mean high water.

Sea Girt, NJ, 1896, 4th order. Red brick Victorian house with lantern tower on roof. Used to guide shipping into and out of New York harbor. It contained the first radio fog beacon in the U.S. Open periodically, free, normally used for civic functions. Bathing beach, rest rooms and park benches nearby. Beacon Blvd & Ocean Rd., Sea Girt, NJ. 201-449-9337.

Egg Island or Maurice River Range, NJ, 1898, two 4th order range lights at opposite ends of wooden walkways with a 2-story wood clapboard frame keepers' dwelling in center. Two of three lights marked the approaches to the Maurice (pronounced Morris) River (see East Point, NJ, 1857). The range lights marked the west side of the Maurice River Cove. Built on pilings over the marsh, the station could only be accessed by boat. The complete station included the necessary boat house in addition to the keepers' dwelling and oil house. The range lights were automated around 1930 and the keepers removed.

Appendix I - Lighthouses of New Jersey and Delaware Bay

The 1939 Light List describes them as: In marsh of west side of mouth of river. Range Front, flashing white 1 sec, 15 ft above water. Range Rear, Occ.. (Occulting.. a steady light totally eclipsed at intervals) white, 2 sec, 0.2 mile 346 degrees from front light, 34 ft above water. An unknown arsonist burned the keepers' house, April 27, 1958.

Elbow of Cross Ledge, DE, 1907, a steel skeleton tower and automatic beacon marks the Elbow of Cross Ledge. The government built this to replace the abandoned lighthouse that originally marked Cross Ledge (see Cross Ledge).

Cross Ledge, 1910, now an abandoned concrete-filled pier that once held a lighthouse marking the southern end of Cross Ledge. In 1901, a gas buoy marked this shoal. By 1910, a lighthouse described as a "red brick dwelling on a brown cylindrical pier," marked the Ledge. Like its sisters in the bay, the service had to rebuild it several times. Finally an ocean-going ship rammed it in the 1950s, doing irreparable damage. Shortly after the incident, the service abandoned the site and demolished the lighthouse structure leaving only an unmarked caisson.

Miah Maull Shoal, NJ, 1913, this lighthouse marks a shoal named after a river pilot who wrecked and drowned here in a storm. Congress appropriated funds for its construction in 1906, 1907, and 1911. Similar in shape to the Brandywine Shoal Lighthouse, the Light List describes it as a "cast iron pier filled with concrete which supports a 3-story circular dwelling of cast iron. A shipyard assembled the pier on shore, towed it out to the site, and sunk it in place on 187 14-inch oak piles. An active light, it continues to guide ships into the Port of Philadelphia. Located in the bay. Not open to the public.

Highlights for New Jersey Lighthouses

Oldest continuously operating lighthouse in the United States, Sandy Hook. Began operation in 1764.

First true "outside" lightship in America, anchored in the open sea instead of in a bay or inlet, entered service off Sandy Hook, N.J. in 1823.

First Fresnel lenses in America installed at Navesink Twin Lights in 1840. Commander Matthew C. Perry, at the direction of Congress, brought the first two lenses from France into the U.S. They were installed at Navesink.

First screwpile lighthouse in America, Brandywine Shoal in the Delaware Bay 1850.

First lighthouse with a steam driven fog siren, installed at Sandy Hook East Beacon in 1868.

First use of mineral oil (kerosene) in a First-Order lighthouse in the U.S., Navesink converted in 1883.

Most unique lighthouse in the U.S. is the Statue of Liberty on Bedloe Island, NJ. The statue was dedicated Oct. 28, 1886 and turned over to the Lighthouse Board on Nov. 22nd. The board had the metal sides of the torch cut away, installed glass, a lamp, and a lens.

First incandescent lamp to be installed in a U.S. lighthouse, Sandy Hook Lighthouse converted in 1889.

First electrically powered primary light in the U.S. Installed in 1898. Although harbor lights had already been equipped with electric lamps, the bulbs were not powerful enough for first-order coastal lights.

First wireless telegraph message received at Twin Lights on September 3, 1899. Guglielmo Marconi transmitted the message at sea aboard the S.S. Ponce, a ship of the "Great White Fleet" honoring Dewey.

Most powerful light in the U.S. was the electric arc and bivalve lens installed at Navesink in 1920. It produced 25-million candlepower. They cut it back to 9-million candlepower in 1931 because of local complaints.

First radio fog beacons in U.S. were installed at the Sea Girt Lighthouse and the Ambrose Lightship in 1921.

First sodium vapor lamp in the U.S. installed at the Cape May Lighthouse in 1934.

INDEX

1823 Lighthouse, 13–14, **14,** 79
   location, **93**
   structure and size, **8,** 13
1847 Lighthouse, 15–18, **17,** 79
   catoptric reflectors, **16,** 16–17
   cut-off base left standing, 15, **15,** 18, 39, **44,** 44–45, 48, 80, 92
   demolition in 1862, 18
   inspection in 1851, 16
   location, **93**
   structure and size, **8,** 15

Absecon Inlet (NJ) lighthouse, 20, 106
aerobeacons, 60
Army Corps of Engineers, 20, 22, 78

Bache, Hartman, 22, 91
Bailey, John, 64
Bailie, Samuel, 74
Barnegat Inlet (NJ) lighthouse, 20, 26, 105
beach erosion, 14, 73–76, **75, 76, 93**
beacon, rotating, 37–38, **38,** 59, 84
Belanger, J., 94
Benstead, Elwood E., 95
birds, protection against, 32
Bradway, Steve, 68–69
Brandywine Shoal (NJ) lighthouse, **104,** 104–105, 111
Breakwater (DE) lighthouse, 108–109
brickwork, 23–24
Budd, James, 82
bunker, World War II, 58, **58,** 74–75
Bureau of Lighthouses, 57, 81, 86
Burgio, Jane, **63**

Cain, Edward, **63**
Cape Charles (VA) lighthouse, 17, 87, 100
Cape Fear (NC) lighthouse, 17, 87, 100
Cape Hatteras (NC) lighthouse, 17, 87, 100
Cape Henlopen (DE) Lighthouse, 10–12, **13,** 78, 82, 102
   destruction by erosion, **103**
   improvements ordered, 17, 87, 100
Cape Henry (VA) lighthouse, 17, 87, 100
Cape Lookout (NC) Lighthouse, 17, 87, 100
Cape May County Historical Museum, 35, 36, 82
Cape May Point State Park, beach erosion of, 74, **76**
Cape May, Delaware Bay & Sewell's Point Railroad, 36, 40, 42, 74, 81
Cape May, historical importance of, 10–11
Cape Romain (SC) lighthouse, 17, 87, 100
Carroll, Thomas, 5, 61, **63**
catadioptric prisms, 33. *see also* Fresnel lens
catoptric light, 16, **16,** 99
Centennial Exhibition of 1876, 42–43, 80, 92, 102
Civil Service System, keepers as part of, 51
Cleveland, Grover, 51
Coast Guard. *see* U.S. Coast Guard
concrete ship, 58, 74, 81
cottages. *see* dwellings, keepers'
Coxe, Daniel, 82
Cross Ledge (DE) lighthouse, 110
Crowell, A. E. D., 94
Cumings, L., 94
curtains, protection of lens by, 32

Decatur, Stephen, 75–76, 78
Delaware Bay, lighthouses of, 102–110
double-wall tower design, 26–27
drop tube for guide pulley, 28, **29,** 35
dwellings, keepers', **19,** 45–47, 90–91
   fire in 1968, 46–47, **47,** 56, 60, 82
   lightning strike of 1891, 29
   third added (1902), 39, **42, 45,** 45–46

East Point (NJ) lighthouse, **106,** 106–107
Edmonds, Enos, 95
Egg Island (NJ) lighthouse, **109,** 109–110
Eldredge, William B., 95
electrification of beacon, 36–37, 57, 81
Eldridge, Lewis G., 95
Eppler, Larry, **63**
Europe, early lighthouses in, 98

112

Everingham, Geo. W., 94

First Order Lens. *see* Fresnel lens
flash panels, 31, 33, **33, 34,** 35. *see also* Fresnel lens
floor, radial tongue-and-groove, 28, **29,** 71–72
fog beacons, 109, 111
Foster, Ann (Hughes), **53**
Foster, Douglas, 94
Foster, Downes E., **50,** 52, **53,** 94
    experience, lack of, 50, 88
    reappointment as keeper, 53
    recordkeeping by, 18
Foster, Reuben, 94
Foster, Sam L., 94
foundation, 26
Fourteen Foot Bank (DE) lighthouse, **107,** 108, **108**
Franklin, W. B., 22, 91
Fresnel lens
    bullseye lens, 37–38, **38**
    first-order lens, 17, 31, **32,** 32–35, **33, 34,** 72, 111
Fresnel, Augustin, 18, 33, 87, 100
Funck hydraulic float lamp, 35–36, **36**
fundraising. *see* restoration

Givler, Henry, 83
Global Positioning System (GPS), 60
Gregory, William C., 22, 52, 53, 79–80, 94
grounds and facilities, 39–48, **42, 44.** *see also* dwellings, keepers'
    miliary use of, 57–58
    oil house, **45,** 47–48, 70, 80, 84
    privies, **48,** 72
    sidewalks, brick, **55,** 55–56, 72
    survey of (1889), **41**
guide pulley for lens weight, 28, **29,** 35

Hall, James F., 64
Hamilton, Alexander, 10

Hand, Japhet, 12
Hand, Thomas (2nd), 11, 78, 82
Harbor of Refuge (DE) lighthouse, 105–106, **106**
Henderson, William, 94
Henry, Michael, 68
Hereford Inlet (NJ) lighthouse, 107–108
historic significance, recognition of, 60–61, 82
Howland, Capt., 88–89
Hughes, Edward, 95
Hughes, William J., **63,** 64
Hurley, James, **63**
hydraulic float lamp, 35–36

inspection of lighthouses (1851), 16
International Chimney Corp., 65, 66–67

Jeacocks, William, 82
Jupiter Inlet, lighthouse at, 20

keepers. *see also specific names*
    duties, 29, 35, 51–52, 56
    dwellings (*see* dwellings, keepers')
    political appointment of, 49–50
    rosters of, 52, 94–95
    salaries, 52, 94–95
kerosene, as lamp fuel, 35, 80
Kimball, Sumner I., 100

lamps, 35–37. *see also* lantern; light
    bulb replacement, automatic, 37, 57, 81
    Funck hydraulic float, 35–36, **36**
    oil vapor, 36, 81
    rotating beacon, 37–38, **38,** 59, 84
    sodium vapor, 103, 111
lantern, **24, 30,** 31–38, 84. *see also* Fresnel lens; lamps; light
    restoration, 67
    structure, 31–32
LaPaute, Henry, 33
lens, Fresnel. *see* Fresnel lens
Lewis, Winslow, 99–100

113

Index

Lifesaving Station, 42, **44,** 92
    Coast Guard's use of, 59
    destruction of, 44, 82
light. *see also* lamps; lantern
    aerobeacons, 60
    extinguishment during war, 22, 57, 81
Lighthouse Board, 16–18, 45, 50, 86, 87
Lighthouse Committee, 62, 64–65, 69
Lighthouse Service, 16, 35, 37, 42
    consolidation with U.S. Coast Guard, 100
    establishment, 78, 99
    naming of lighthouses by, 96–97
lightning strike (1891), 29
lookout platform, 58, 82

MAC. *see* Mid-Atlantic Center for the Arts
Marshall, Greg, **63**
masonry, 23–24
Masonry Preservation Group, 71–72, 83
Maurice River Range (NJ) lighthouse, 109–110
Meade, George Gordon, 20, **20,** 22, 35
Miah Maull Shoal (NJ) lighthouse, 110, **110**
Mid-Atlantic Center for the Arts (MAC)
    establishment (1970), 82
    lighthouse management by, 5, 61–72, 76
Middleton, Nathan, 15, 79, 88
Middleton, Samuel, 15, 79, 88
Mills, Ephraim, 52, 79
Morris Island (SC) lighthouse, 17, 87, 100
museum shop, 48, 62, 70

naming, inconsistent, 83, 96–97
Navesink (NJ), Twin Towers of, 105, **105,** 111
New Jersey Dept. of Transportation, 65, 71, 83
New Jersey Historic Trust, 65, 71, 83
New Jersey, lighthouses of, 102–111

oil house, **45,** 47–48, 70, 80, 84
oil vapor lamp, 36, 81

Palmer, Ada, **23,** 32, 36, **55,** 55–56, 56
Palmer, Florence, **55**
Palmer, Florence Arabelle ("Belle"), **54,** 55, **55,** 81
Palmer, Harry, 48, 52, **52,** 54–56, **55, 56,** 81, 95

Palmer, Ida, 55
Perry, Matthew C., 18
Peterson, Roger Tory, 32
pharology, defined, 20, 98
Pleasanton, Stephen, 50, 79, 87
privies, **48,** 72
Pusey, Jno. S., 95
Pyne, Jonathan, 78

rain, infiltration by, 70–71
range of visibility, 84
Raynolds, William F., 22, 91
Reeves, John, 94
Repp, Dorothy, **55**
Repp, Ruth, **55**
restoration, 61–72, **66, 71**
    fundraising, 62–65, 71
    opening ceremonies, **61,** 63–64, 69–70, 82–83
roof, restoration of, 67–71, **68, 69, 70**
Rumsey, Charles, **34**

Sandy Hook (NJ) lighthouse, 10, 22, 102, 111
Schmierer, Charles, **55**
Schmierer, Doris, **55**
Schmierer, Floyd K., 95
Schmierer, Kenneth, **55**
Sea Girt (NJ) lighthouse, 109, 111
Sea Grove Association, 80, 92
Ship John Shoal (NJ) lighthouse, 102–103, **104**
sidewalks, brick, **55,** 55–56, 72
size of structure, **8,** 84, 90
Snyder, Jacob A., 94
South Cape May, loss to beach erosion, 74
sperm whale oil, as lamp fuel, 35, 79
stairs, spiral, **24,** 25, 27, **27, 28,** 72
Statue of Liberty, as beacon, 108, 111
steps. *see* stairs, spiral
Stevens, Ezekiel, 52–53, 79
Stevens, Lewis D., 79, 94–95
Stilwell, Samuel, 52–54, 80, 94–95
Stites, Howard, 94–95
Stites, John, 40, 78–79, 92
suicide by visitor in 1995, 70, 83
sunlight, protection of lens from, 32

telephone system, 29
Thornton, Eileen, **63**
tower, lighthouse, structural elements of, **24,** 26–27
towers, military lookout, 58, **59**
trolley, **39,** 42, 73–74
Twin Towers of Navesink (NJ), 18, 105, **105**

U.S. Coast Guard
    establishment in 1915, 81
    management of lighthouse by, 57, 59–61, 64
ultraviolet rays, protection of lens from, 32
uniforms, keepers', 51, **52**

ventilation of lantern, importance of, 32
vestibule, **24,** 25–26
visibility, of beacon, 84

Wanamaker, John, 80
watch room, **24,** 28–29, **31**
Watson and Henry Associates, 62, 65, 82
Whilldin, Alexander, 40, **40,** 79–80, 91
Whilldin, Jane G. (Stites), 79
Williams, Otis James Franklin, 95
Wilson, Edwin, 95
Woolson, Caleb Swain, 52–54, 81, 95

FOOTNOTES

1. Folk Song Encyclopedia, Vol II, Jerry Silverman, Pg. 264, Chappell Music Co., NY.

2.. The Works of Alexander Hamilton, comprising his correspondence, and his political and official writings, edited by John C. Hamilton, Page 23, Vol. IV, New York. John F. Trow, printer. 1851.

3. America's Lighthouses, an Illustrated History, Francis Ross Holland, Jr. Dover Publications, Inc. New York, pg. 11, 77

4. Cape May Court House deed dated September 23, 1785.

5. New London, Iowa Town History, New London Centennial, Hand genealogy.

6. America's Lighthouses, Holland, pg.77.

7. Fourth District Engineers Report 20 March 1878, paragraph describing history of site.

8. Form 152, (government document) Amount of Appropriations, &c., May 4, 1780, to June 30, 1862, "Reference to Stats. At Large," Vol 3, pg. 698 and 780.

9. Lighthouse List for 1849 and 1851 describing first lighthouse.

10. Ho! For Cape Island, Robert Crozier Alexander, self publ. 1956, pg. 43 (recounting a visit to the lighthouse in 1823).

11. Ho! For Cape Island, Robert Crozier Alexander, self publ. 1956, pg. 47.

12. Report on Lighthouses, 1852; Cape May Inspection Report dated June 25, 1851, pg. 193.

13. Form 152, (government document) Amount of Appropriations, &c., May 4, 1780 to June 30, 1862, "Reference to Stats At Large," Vol 11, pg. 223.

14. Lighthouse Board Annual Report. 1862.

15. Keeper's Notes, From the Curator of the Cape May Lighthouse, Issue #3/June, 1995, Diane L. Cripps, Curator.

16. The Life and Letters of George Gordon Meade - 2 vol sct. Charles Scribner's Sons, New York: 1913.

17. Lighthouse Board Annual Report; 1891.

18. Cape May County Historical & Genealogical Museum, 504 U.S. Rte 9, Cape May Court House, NJ 08210; 609-465-3535.

19. Fourth District Engineers Report 20 March 1878, 5th paragraph.

20. Fourth District Engineers description of the Lighthouse, March 20, 1878.

21. Fourth District Engineers description of the Lighthouse, March 20, 1878.

22. Deed recorded May 1st AD 1858 in the Clerks Office of the County of Cape May, NJ at Cape May Court House, book No. 26, pages 635 & 636.

23. Fourth District Engineers Description of Lighthouse Tower, Buildings, and Premises at Cape May Light Station, New Jersey, July 26 and November 19, 1907; item 14.

24. Fourth District Engineers Description of the Light-House Tower, March 20, 1878.

25. Lighthouse Board Annual Reports; 1879, 1880, 1896, 1897, 1898, 1899, 1900.

26. Fourth District Engineers Description of Light-House Tower, Buildings, and Premises at Cape May Light Station, New Jersey, July 26 and November 19, 1907: items 142, 144, and 145.

27. For a complete listing of all known keepers at the Cape May Lighthouse, see Appendix F.

28. Ho! for Cape Island, Robert Crozier, self-published, 1956. Page 52

29. *Cape May Herald*, October. 1, 1903

30. Department of Commerce, letter dated June 29, 1933 from the Chief of Appointment Division.

31. From an Army veteran stationed at the gun emplacement during World War II and reported to Lighthouse guide Charles Rumsey.

32. Michael C. Henry, P.E., A.I.A., P.P., Penelope S. Watson, A.I.A., 12 North Pearl St, Bridgeton, NJ 08302, 856-451-1779.

33. Fourth District Engineers Description of Light-House Tower, Buildings, and Premises at Cape May Light Station, New Jersey, July 26 and November 19, 1907.

34. Joseph J. Jakubik, Project Mgr., International Chimney Corp., P.O. Box 260, 55 S. Long St., Buffalo, NY 14231-0260

35. Masonry Preservation Group, Inc. 706 West Maple Avenue., Merchantville, NJ 08109, 609-663-4158

36. *Cape May Star & Wave*, Thursday, July 4, 1985, pg. 20, Eleanor Graham Foster.

37. Scheyichbi And The Strand, An Account of Recent Events at Sea Grove, by Edward S. Wheeler, Pg. 82, Press of J.B. Lippincott & Co. Philadelphia, 1876.

38. Department of Commerce letter to Elwood E. Benstead regarding his conclusion of service, dated April 10, 1922.

39. Appointment registers for lighthouse personnel serving in the area from New York thru Va. 1840-1910, (roll 2 National Archives Microcopy M-1373).

40. The first two lighthouses only had one keeper. After 1859, two assistants worked with the keeper.

41. Report on Lighthouses, 1852; Cape May Inspection Report

42. *Cape May Herald*, Oct. 1903.

43. The Keeper's Log, Winter 1989, Roman Lighthouses, Wayne C. Wheeler, Pg . 22 &24.

44. The Keeper's Log, Winter 1989, Roman Lighthouses, Pg. 25.

45. The Keeper's Log, Fall 1990, Brazier-Lighthouses, D.B. Hague, Pg. 24.

46. The Works of Alexander Hamilton, comprising his correspondence, and his political and official writings, edited by John C. Hamilton, Page 23, Vol. IV, New York. John F. Trow, printer. 1851.

47. Hgt = height of tower, fp = focal plane (height of the light above mean sea level)

About the Author

John Bailey was born in Millville, New Jersey, but grew up in Fort Lauderdale, FL. He sailed the high seas as a First Class Sonarman with the Navy destroyer service for 8-1/2 years, leaving the Navy after an intense tour of duty in the Western Pacific during the Vietnam War. His love of the sea and the years spent upon it had laid the groundwork for his interest in lighthouses - the first thing he remembers the ship's lookout siting when returning to port and home.

After his Navy tours, John wrote user manuals for computer manufacturers, National Cash Register in Dayton, Ohio, and digital equipment corp. in Boston, Mass. Growing bored with the corporate life (suits and ties), he and his wife, Nancy, began exploring the idea of promoting another of his interests, leather crafting. They worked after corporate hours and traveled to craft shows throughout New England, New York, and Pennsylvania as the Back Bay Workshop. Finally, they decided to open a store-front shop and found their way to Cape May. In 1976, they opened the Baileywicke Leather Shop on the Washington Street Mall. Today, he is a member of the prestigious Guild of Master Craftsmen in Sussex, Great Britain.

John is a past-president of MAC and presently (2000) chairman of the Lighthouse Committee. He is a District Inspector member of the U. S. Lighthouse Society, and an active member of the Cape May Kiwanis who meet in the original Sewell's Point, Cape May Lifesaving Station building.

When the Mid-Atlantic Center for the Arts (MAC) assumed responsibility for the Cape May Lighthouse, they asked John to join the Lighthouse Committee as the resident shopkeeper who could help them set up a museum shop. At the first meeting, someone observed that they should have a "Save the Lighthouse" t-shirt to sell at the museum shop. John raised his hand and agreed to design a logo for the shirt. Those t-shirts have raised thousands of dollars for the restoration effort. Someone else at the meeting mentioned that they should have an informational pamphlet or booklet to give or sell to the visitors to the lighthouse. John, considered his writing background in Dayton and Boston, again raised his hand and volunteered to write the booklet.

That booklet has since become this book, *The Sentinel of the Jersey Cape*.

Sentinel of the Jersey Cape
The Story of the Cape May Lighthouse

Production Credits

Book Design: Kathy Motak Singel, Singel Design

Indexing: Ann Brennan Day

Production Editor: Jennifer Brownstone Kopp

Proofreading: Nancy Bailey

Cover and Dust Jacket Photography: Corey Gilbert

Color Separations and Prepress: Joseph Roman, Todd Linn (DCI)

Printing: Digital Color Image, Pennsauken, NJ

Finishing: Short Run Bindery, Medford, NJ

Cape Publishing, Inc.
Cape May, New Jersey
609-898-4500

www.capepublishing.com
www.capemay.com